CUBA *in the* 1970s

D0874829

CUBA
in the
1970s

Pragmatism and Institutionalization

Carmelo Mesa-Lago

UNIVERSITY OF NEW MEXICO PRESS

Albuquerque

© The University of New Mexico Press, 1974. All rights reserved.
Manufactured in the United States of America.
Library of Congress Catalog Card Number LC 74-83385
International Standard Book Number ISBN 0-8263-0348-X
  (clothbound)
International Standard Book Number ISBN 0-8263-0350-1
  (paperbound)
First Edition

Second Printing, 1976

*To the new Cuban generations
both inside and outside of the nation
with the hope that their paths
will converge in the future.*

Contents

Tables

Preface

The Cuban Revolution is a phenomenon in such flux that to write about it always involves a risk: what appears as solid after some years of accumulated evidence can dramatically change in a few weeks or even days. Fifteen years after Fidel Castro's takeover, one thing at least is clear: the revolutionary process has not moved steadily and in the same direction but has been erratic, submitted to numerous changes in philosophy and policy. Five stages of the Revolution can now be distinguished: 1959–1960—liquidation of the capitalist system; 1961–1963—introduction of socialist institutions following the pre-reform Soviet system; 1963–1965—discussion of and experimentation with alternative systems of socialist organization; 1966–1970—adoption and radicalization of the idealistic Sino-Guevarist system; and, since 1970—return to pragmatism and the more conventional post-reform Soviet system.

I have already devoted considerable time and space elsewhere to describing and analyzing the first four stages of the Revolution (1959–1970) and, hence, this book will not duplicate my previous writings. It will concentrate on the current stage, specifically on the four years elapsed from mid-1970 to mid-1974. Very little has been written on this stage, mostly journalistic articles which describe fragmentally specific facets of the process thus lacking an overall, cohesive analysis of it.

My contention is that the Revolution has come of age and, learning from its mistakes and under Soviet influence, has become increasingly pragmatic and institutionalized. The former personalistic-charismatic regime is being transformed by delegation of power from the "maximum leader" to technocrats, separation of functions of the administration, the party, and the armed forces, and revitalization of the party, the unions, and other mass organizations. The romanticism of the 1960s has apparently come to an end, resulting in disillusion

for permanent revolutionaries and devoted idealists. Thus a noticeable decline of interest in Cuba is reported from university campuses
in the United States and abroad. Fidel Castro is no longer a critic of
the Soviet Union but its most conspicuous defender in the Third
World. The days of sending armed expeditions to establish guerrilla
foci that would transform the Andean range into the Sierra Maestra
of South America are over. Today Cuba is busily working out trade,
diplomatic, and anti-hijacking agreements with as many Latin
American countries as possible. The appealing, quixotic attempt to
skip the transitional phase of socialism and rapidly create a "New
Man" in an egalitarian communistic society through the development of consciousness, the use of moral incentives, and labor
mobilization has been quietly halted. The talk of the day in Cuba is
economic incentives, wage differentials, and building the material
base through the use of cost-benefit analysis and raising capital
efficiency and labor productivity. The uniqueness of the Cuban
Revolution, so much praised in the past by Sartre, has gradually
dulled and the more conventional features of socialism "a la Eastern
Europe" appear increasingly stronger in the island.

And yet the Revolution is there, surviving innumerous confronta-
tions and crises. The Cubans reportedly feel that the worst is behind
and that there are better days ahead. The obsessive mobilization and
ascetic frugality of the 1960s have receded and life seems easier now.
Instead of trying to solve all the problems of the continent at once,
Cuban leaders and bureaucrats have realistically turned inward to
tackle daily domestic problems with more patience, caution, and
rationality. The satisfaction of basic needs like food, clothing, and
housing is still the most difficult problem facing them but there have
been some improvements in this area since four years ago. The new
stage, however, has negative aspects such as the tightening control
over ideology, education, and culture, while the promised democratization of unions and workers' participation in decision making have
to be tested in the immediate future.

Research for this book required a systematic and exhaustive review
of Cuban magazines, newspapers, and radio dispatches, and of the
growing specialized literature published in Cuban *ad hoc* reports and

scientific journals during 1970–73. My work as editor of the *Cuban Studies Newsletter* published by the Center for Latin American Studies, University of Pittsburgh, was of great help because it gave me exposure to thousands of items that, since 1970, are annually classified by the CSN. In addition, through exchanges of the *CSN*, we obtain rare statistical bulletins from Cuba and technical reports most of which are not available elsewhere in the United States. I usually used *Granma Weekly Review* for the official English version of the Cuban leaders' speeches. When the latter were not reproduced in that publication or the speech had special significance, I resorted to one of the two Cuban daily newspapers *(Granma* and *Juventud Rebelde)* and did the translation myself.

Segments of this book have appeared earlier in the following articles of mine: "The Sovietization of the Cuban Revolution: Its Consequences for the Western Hemisphere," *World Affairs*136 (Summer 1973), pp. 3–35; "Castro's Domestic Course," *Problems of Communism*22 (September-October 1973), pp. 27–38; and "Conversion of the Cuban Economy to Soviet Orthodoxy," *Journal of Economic Issues*8 (March 1974), pp. 41–65. I am grateful to the editors of these journals for granting permission to use materials from the cited articles in this book. My appreciation also to Professor Edward González, from UCLA, who supplied materials for and commented on chapter 1; to Professor Lourdes Casal, from Rutgers University, who shared with me many of her impressions from a visit to Cuba in the summer of 1973; to Dr. Heinrich Brunner, from Freien Universität Berlin, who made rigorous criticisms of chapter 2 and gave me insights from his visit to Cuba in late 1972; and to Professor Nelson Valdés, from Louisiana State University, who supplied some materials for chapter 3. The responsibility for what is said here of course is only mine. The book would not have been published without the substantial help received from : Shirley Kregar, Carolyn Wilson, and Donna Bobin from the University of Pittsburgh's Center for Latin American Studies who edited and/or typed the manuscript several times; Eduardo Lozano, the Latin American bibliographer of the University of Pittsburgh who was, as always, generous with his time and extremely helpful with his knowledge of the Cuban collection; and to Carl Mora from the University of New Mexico Press who encouraged me to put together this book and did the final editing.

Each of my last three books on Cuba has been preceded by the birth of a new daughter, this one by Helenita. She, as well as Elizabeth and Ingrid, and my always cheerful wife Elena have filled with love the time that the book robbed from them. In return I offer this book to them, with my love increased for their precious contribution.

C. M. L.

Abbreviations of Cuban Institutions Referred to in this Book
with Date of Founding

ANAP	National Association of Small Farmers, 1961
CDR	Committees for the Defense of the Revolution, 1960
CTC	Confederation of Cuban Workers, 1939
EJT	Youth Army of Work, 1973
FAR	Revolutionary Armed Forces, 1961
FMC	Federation of Cuban Women, 1960
ICAIC	Cuban Institute of Cinema Arts, 1959
INRA	National Institute of Agrarian Reform, 1959
JUCEPLAN	Central Planning Board, 1960
MININ	Ministry of Interior, 1961
OLAS	Organization of Latin American Solidarity, 1967
OPP	Organs of Popular Power, 1974
ORI	Integrated Revolutionary Organizations 1961–1963
PCC	Communist Party of Cuba, 1965
PSP	Socialist Popular Party, 1925–1961
PURS	United Party of the Socialist Revolution, 1963–1965
SMO	Compulsory Military Service, 1963
SS	Compulsory Social Service, 1973
UMAP	Military Units to Aid Production, 1964–1973
UNEAC	National Union of Writers and Artists of Cuba, 1961
UJC	Young Communist League, 1962

1

A New Stage of the Cuban Revolution: The 1970s

Since the triumph of the insurrection against the Batista regime in 1959, the Cuban Revolution has passed through five distinct phases. In the 1970s the Soviet Union has been increasing its influence over Cuba through personal and institutional channels of both a political and economic nature.

Table 1 presents a concise but global picture of the principal features of each of the five stages of the Revolution from 1959 to 1973. The following sections will not review all of these features but will attempt to pinpoint the currents of thought that promoted changes and shaped the various stages.[1]

Five Stages of the Revolution, 1959-1973

The first stage of the Revolution (1959–1960) lacked a defined ideology, but there were statist, populist, anti-market, consumption-ist, and nationalistic tendencies. The new revolutionary elite undertook the systematic liquidation or control of the most powerful prerevolutionary pressure groups: the army, political parties, unions, and farmers' and professional associations. These were substituted in many cases by new institutions which strongly supported the Revolution such as the Rebel Army, the militia, and the Committees

1

TABLE 1

Features of Five Stages in the First Fifteen Years of the Cuban Revolution

Features	Liquidation of Pre-revolutionary Institutions 1959-1960	Attempt to Introduce the Soviet System 1961-1963	Debate of and Experimentation with Alternative Systems 1963-1966	Adoption and Radicalization of the Sino-Guevarist System 1966-1970	Return to Pragmatism and the Soviet System 1970-1973
Development Strategy	Industrialization, anti-sugar bias	Ibid; sharp decline in sugar output, delays in industrial development	Return to sugar, heavy industrialization postponed	Emphasis on sugar reaches climax in 1970; record crop but target is not fulfilled and output declines in rest of economy	Deemphasis on sugar; targets set at levels that can be reached without affecting other sectors
Ownership of Means of Production	Increasing collectivization with momentum in late 1960; agriculture is exception with predominance of private farms and cooperatives	Agricultural cooperatives transformed into state farms in 1962; reduction in private farm sector in 1963 and procurement quotas ("acopio") imposed upon farmers	No significant changes	State ownership is completed (except for 1/3 of agriculture) in 1968 during the "Revolutionary Offensive"	Pressure on private farmers to expand their sales to and work for the state
Planning Model	Economic disorganization and lack of controls; gradual reduction of market	Attempt to introduce highly centralized, physical planning with the aid of Soviet and Czech technicians	Change in development strategy and problems with central planning induce experimentation with decentralization techniques	Long-run, central "macro" plan substituted by short-run, loose "micro" (sectorial) plans	Return to long-run central planning with aid of computer techniques
Financing Method	Mixture of private (rapidly declining) and budgetary (in state sector)	Mainly budgetary, but problems with capital efficiency	Experiments with self-financing in 1/3 of state enterprises, particularly in agriculture and foreign trade	Budgetary throughout the economy, except private farms	Probably a partial return to self-financing
Consumption and Capital Accumulation	Emphasis on consumption (wage increases, free social services); capital accumulation declines sharply	Individual consumption restricted, rationing begins in 1962; recuperation of prerevolutionary investment rate	Emphasis on capital accumulation continues	Capital accumulation is escalated reaching a peak in 1968; but there is considerable waste of investment due to inefficient allocation and use of capital	Moderate reduction in capital accumulation and increase in consumption; emphasis on capital efficiency
Incentives and Egalitarianism	Material incentives, mainly of an individual nature, reduction in extreme inequalities	Decline in material-individual incentives, emphasis on collective incentives, mostly material; rationing is an equalizer	Limited experimentation with individual-material incentives, e.g., wage differentials, awards in kind, production bonuses	Drastic reduction of individual-material incentives; enormous emphasis on moral stimuli and egalitarianism to forge the unselfish "New Man"	Previous excesses on moral incentives and egalitarianism are criticized; return to individual-material incentives

Criteria for Manager Selection	Alienated managers and technicians who fled the country or were fired are replaced by loyal but incompetent revolutionaries	Attempt to train managerial personnel in Cuba or abroad—principally in Eastern Europe and U.S.S.R.	Increased emphasis on raising managerial and technical skills	Anti-bureaucracy campaign reaches climax; revolutionary zeal takes predominance over expertise	Emphasis in training returns; loyal but incompetent managers have to acquire skills or will be fired
Employment and Labor Productivity	Expansion of employment in agriculture and services; labor productivity stagnant	Full employment practically achieved but largely through artificial job creation; labor productivity declines	Attempt to transfer labor surplus to agriculture and to increase labor productivity by introducing Soviet system of work quotas and wage scales	Work-quota system is neglected; labor productivity reaches lowest ebb; manpower deficit is aggravated by labor absenteeism	Reintroduction of work quotas, increase in labor productivity, reduction of labor absenteeism, a few unemployment pockets appear
Financial Equilibrium (inflation)	Consumption increases faster than production and imports; depletion of stocks; balance of payments deficit grows	Prices are frozen, rationing is introduced and gradually expanded to cover most consumer goods; the black market appears	The disequilibrium between monetary supply and available consumer goods increases and the black market grows rapidly; this operates as a disincentive for labor	The disequilibrium reaches a record in 1970 when the monetary surplus is almost equal to the population income; labor absenteeism increases to a record	The monetary surplus is reduced to less than half the population income, through price increases and expanded supply of consumer goods
Army and Para-military Bodies	Rebel Army systematically destroys remnants of old army and plays crucial role in implementing agrarian reform; militia founded in late 1959	Ministry of Armed Forces established; army is trained and equipped by the U.S.S.R.; militia is vital in defeating Bay of Pigs invasion	Increasing professionalization of the army; compulsory military service is established in 1963; weapons are taken away from militia and its role declines	Military men take top positions in the party, administration, management; increased militarization of labor through brigades	New ranks introduced in the army which becomes more specialized and reduced in size; militia is being phased out and labor brigades merged into separate agency
Party Development	Only a few political organizations are allowed to function: 26th of July Movement, Student Directorate, and PSP	ORI is integrated by the three political organizations but largely controlled by PSP; purge against sectarianism results in substitution of ORI by PURS, controlled by Castroites	PCC is established in 1965 with top positions in Castroite hands; membership is very small, seldom holds meetings and lacks program	Functions of the administration and the party are fused in practice; a new purge against the "microfaction" (some members of former PSP) is launched in 1968	Separation of administration and party functions; the latter is reorganized, its membership expanded and its first congress announced for 1975
Unions and Other Mass Organizations	Pressures upon unions begin in 1959 and control measures surface in 1960; the Committees for the Defense of the Revolution are founded in 1960	Unions become "transmission belts" of administration; in 1961 private farmers are integrated into ANAP, and in 1962 youth associations into UJC	No significant changes	National congress of unions adheres to the new line; unions are practically substituted by vanguard-worker movement	Elections are held in local unions in 1971 and a national congress in 1973; ANAP and UJC are also reorganized

TABLE 1 continued

Features of Five Stages in the First Fifteen Years of the Cuban Revolution

Features	Liquidation of Pre-revolutionary Institutions 1959-1960	Attempt to Introduce the Soviet System 1961-1963	Debate of and Experimentation with Alternative Systems 1963-1966	Adoption and Radicalization of the Sino-Guevarist System 1966-1970	Return to Pragmatism and the Soviet System 1970-1973
Mobilization Techniques	Big rallies in support of government decisions and policies; mobilization is basically political	Labor mobilization begins in 1962 ("voluntary labor") to help in sugar harvest and other crops due to manpower deficit	Labor mobilization increases but more sophisticated techniques are used to increase its productivity	Labor mobilization increases dramatically, both for economic and educational reasons (development of consciousness) reaching a peak in 1968-70; productivity is neglected	Labor mobilization is gradually reduced; voluntary labor is only allowed when its productivity is assured beforehand
Control Over Education and Culture	General freedom in spite of numerous incidents and controversies	Private schools and universities are closed; government policy is defined as: within the Revolution everything, outside of it nothing; UNEAC is founded	Many "deviant" writers and intellectuals are sent to labor camps, but the measure is later reversed	Increased militancy is required from writers; several of them are officially critized by army and government officials	The Cultural and Educational Congress of 1971 introduces a more rigid and dogmatic line; conflict with foreign intellectuals
Relations with The U.S.S.R.	Reestablishment of relations; the U.S.S.R. grants credits and takes part of the former U.S. sugar quota	The U.S.S.R. becomes Cuba's main trade partner and creditor; influx of Soviet technicians; first confrontation in 1962 due to Missile Crisis	New accommodation; Castro travels twice to the U.S.S.R.; Guevara steps out; long-term economic and trade agreement between the two countries for 1965-70	New confrontation due to divergent ideologies, economic practices and foreign policy; U.S.S.R. reduces oil supply and Castro purges former PSP members; beginning of new accommodation with Cuba supporting Soviet invasion of Czechoslovakia	Improvement of relations climaxes with two visits of Castro to the U.S.S.R. and Brezhnev's visit to Cuba; Soviet-Cuban Commission established, Cuba enters COMECON; long-term economic agreement signed for 1973-75
Exportation of Revolution to Latin America	Ill-prepared expeditions that fail, lack of a clear ideology and strategy	Cuba ousted from OAS and isolated from Western Hemisphere; Cuban support to guerrillas increases; conflicts with communist parties	Compromising attitude with communist parties in Latin America; agreement on a few countries to which the revolution should be exported	Tricontinental conference and OLAS established; theory of the guerrilla foco as the only way to revolution officially accepted; Guevara tries it in Bolivia and is killed	The exportation of the Revolution practically ends; non-guerrilla roads to revolution are accepted; relations are reestablished with several Latin American countries

for the Defense of the Revolution. In this stage a few of the political organizations that were active during the insurrection (e.g., the 26th of July Movement, the Student Directorate) plus the prerevolutionary Communist party (Popular Socialist Party: PSP) and had accepted Castro's leadership were allowed to function. All important decisions, however, were made by the new government elite who mobilized huge political rallies in their support. There was expanding collectivization of the means of production and a concomitant reduction in market forces. The latter were not substituted by planning and central orders, partly because of the lack of a clear economic program and due to the alienation of former managers and technicians usually replaced by enthusiastic but unskilled revolutionaries. The net result of this situation was widespread economic disorganization. The leaders, however, had a firm commitment to expand employment and raise the living standards of the low-income strata of the population. This goal was achieved at the cost of a drastic curtailment of capital accumulation which in turn affected the viability of other goals such as the elimination of sugar monoculture through rapid industrialization and agricultural diversification. Profoundly nationalistic, the Revolution confronted U.S. interests while reestablishing diplomatic relations and expanding trade with the U.S.S.R. and other socialist countries. The prevailing spirit of continental solidarity combined with the absence of a well thought out strategy induced ill-conceived, futile efforts to promote revolution in Latin America.

After the declaration of socialist faith in early 1961, a second stage began (1961–1963) in which an attempt was made to mechanistically apply the system of politico-economic organization and development prevalent at the time in the U.S.S.R. to Cuba. The few revolutionary organizations allowed to operate merged into the ORI (Integrated Revolutionary Organizations), later transformed into PURS (United Party of the Socialist Revolution), the germ of the future Communist party. The vacuum of the market was intended to be filled by a centralized system of planning and technical aid from the Soviet Union. Emphasis was placed on the training of managerial personnel, and the unions became conduits for the orders of the central administration. Curtailment of consumption to increase investment began with the hope of accelerating the industrialization process and generating high rates of economic growth. It was during this stage that Cuba defeated the U.S.-sponsored invasion at the Bay of Pigs, became almost isolated in the Western Hemisphere, increased its efforts to export the Revolution, and moved closer to the U.S.S.R. This warm relationship was suddenly shaken by the Soviet-American understanding in the Missile Crisis of 1962 which, in the official Cuban view, was a Soviet retreat aggravated by the lack of consultation with Cuba. Failures in planning and the development strategy made now skeptical Cuban leaders question the universality of the Soviet system and its applicability to an island plantation economy. Thus the Revolution moved into a third stage (1963–1966) dominated by a lively debate on alternative systems of organization and development strategies.[2]

In that controversy, Ernesto Che Guevara and his followers, influenced by the system of the Maoist "Great Leap Forward," endorsed an idealistic line of thought (departing from more conventional Soviet thought of the 1960s) which presented three main objectives. First was the total elimination of the market or "commodity production" through full collectivization of the means of production, a highly centralized-computerized planning system, central financing of all state enterprises through budgetary appropriations (i.e., non-repayable, interest-free grants, with transfer of all enterprise profits back to the state budget), and the gradual eradication of money and "material incentives." To be successful, the first action had to be paralleled by the creation of an unselfish, self-sacrificing, frugal, fully-socialized, egalitarian human being—the "New Man." This would be attained by raising mass consciousness through education, mobilization, unpaid voluntary labor, and "moral incentives" (e.g., banners, medals, and free social services provided by the state). Such steps, in turn, would facilitate the process of capital accumulation and economic development. The third goal was the exportation of the Cuban revolutionary model to Latin America. This action was urged on by the premise that continental revolution was indispensable for the survival of socialism in Cuba; it was assumed that the rural guerrilla *foco* was the only way to generate this revolution. The Guevarists were openly critical of the U.S.S.R because, according to their criteria, this nation's domestic and foreign policies did not conform with what socialism should be. They were in favor of the principle of permanent revolution, had a distaste for institutionalization, did not elaborate on the role that the party should play, and proclaimed that trade unions were unnecessary.

Confronting Guevara was a moderate pragmatist group led by the economist Carlos Rafael Rodríguez and composed mostly of pro-Soviet members of the prerevolutionary Communist party (PSP). This group, under the influence of Libermanism (publicized and experimented within the U.S.S.R. by Khrushchev and moderately implemented by Brezhnev and Kosygin), advocated three different positions. One was that central planning should also be based in cybernetic and input-output techniques but with some autonomy at the enterprise level and with partial use of market mechanisms. Against the budgetary technique, they introduced self-financing in about one-third of the state enterprises. These received loans from the central bank, loans which earned interest and had to be repaid; in turn, the enterprise could retain a good part of its profits for reinvestment and expansion. A second goal of the group was economic institutionalization based upon an efficient bureaucracy, high labor productivity through the Soviet system of work quotas, and material incentives (e.g., wage differentials, bonuses for over-fulfillment of work quotas, overtime payments, and awards in kind). Thirdly, the group also favored a strong Communist party, Soviet-style unions, close links with the U.S.S.R., and more flexibility in Cuba's foreign relations with Latin America.

For four years, Castro abstained from openly participating in the controversy but cleverly dismissed or sent abroad the leaders of the two opposing groups. Once his path was cleared of potential opponents, he started the fourth stage of the Revolution (mid-1966 to mid-1970) by endorsing Sino-Guevarism although embellished with personalistic Castroite features. For instance, the most important economic decisions were not concentrated in a "scientific and objective" central planning apparatus, but were made by the prime minister and his inner circle of loyalists and implemented through "mini" or sectorial plans. Emphasis on capital accumulation, mobili-zation, moral incentives, egalitarianism, and abolition of money was heavier than in Guevara's scheme. Grandiose output targets were set for the years ahead, including ten million tons of sugar for the harvest of 1970. The army's influence increased enormously and pervaded many facets of society while the party stagnated. (In 1965, still under Soviet influence, the Communist Party of Cuba [PCC] was established but under Castroite control.) In the meantime, Guevara was fighting in Bolivia to transform the Andean mountain range into a Latin American Sierra Maestra, and Cuban-Soviet relations reached their lowest ebb when Castro denounced the U.S.S.R. for limiting the supply of oil to Cuba and imprisoned a group of PSP leaders ("the microfaction") for their alleged anti-governmental activities. The radicalization movement reached a climax in the spring of 1968 with the "Revolutionary Offensive" (in some aspects similar to the Chinese Cultural Revolution), under which the remainder of the private sector was nationalized, mobilization was accentuated, and a record was established in capital accumulation at the cost of sacrificing consumption. Cuba then claimed that it was building communism and was ahead of the U.S.S.R. in communist ownership, the development of consciousness, and egalitarian distribution. Disaster on both the internal and external fronts (Cuba's deteriorating economy and Guevara's death in Bolivia) forced a reconsideration of some of the previous policies, and the Soviet invasion of Czechoslovakia offered the golden opportunity for it.

Castro's endorsement of the invasion, although qualified, facilitated a steady improvement in Cuban-Soviet relations. This accommodation, together with the realization that continental revolution was not possible for the moment, was pivotal in shaping a less idealistic, more compromising foreign policy vis-a-vis Latin America. Hence other roads to revolutionary change—besides that of the guerrilla *foco*—were accepted, such as peaceful elections and military coups. Both the exportation of the Revolution and the aid to revolutionary groups abroad declined gradually. Although externally the revolutionary policy became increasingly moderate, internally Sino-Guevarism continued in operation as the gigantic mobilization for the 1970 sugar crop gained momentum. The Soviet leaders had accurate information on the poor chances for achieving this goal but they abstained from obstructing Castro's chosen strategy. Probably the gains in Cuban foreign policy were enough reward for them at that point, and to exert pressure in internal matters could have once again generated friction. The sugar harvest eventually produced a record 8.5 million tons; this, however, was below the 10 million-ton target and was achieved at the cost of a sharp decline of production in the non-sugar sector and overall economic dislocation. As a result, the Sino-Guevarist model suffered a mortal blow, Castro's prestige and strength were eroded, and the Soviet Union increased its bargaining power.

Since mid-1970, Soviet influence in Cuba has increased considerably shaping a fifth stage of the Revolution with the following features.[3] Externally Cuba has moved closer than ever to the U.S.S.R. and become its chief defender in the Third World against criticism from more revolutionary leftist positions. Diplomatic and/or trade relations have been reestablished with a dozen Latin American countries with divergent socio-politico-economic systems. Internally there is a process of institutionalization characterized by delegation of power from the previously quasi-omnipotent Castro, strengthening of the Communist party, specialization of the army, and reorganization of the unions and other mass organizations. This has been paralleled by the tightening of central controls in ideology, education, and culture. In economics there has been an acknowledgment that the previous policy was too idealistic and that a more realistic, conventional approach is necessary. New policies include the strengthening of the central planning apparatus, the more rational use of capital and manpower to increase productivity, the expansion of material incentives, the drastic reduction in labor mobilization, and the setting of realistic output targets (particularly in sugar).

Increasing Soviet Influence Since 1970

Most specialists on Cuban affairs believe, regardless of their ideological coloration, that since Prime Minister Fidel Castro endorsed the Soviet invasion of Czechoslovakia, the U.S.S.R. has played an increasing role in Cuban affairs, particularly since 1970.[4]

Soviet control has been achieved in various ways. Castro has delegated most economic powers to President Osvaldo Dorticós, a moderate whom the Soviets trust, and to Carlos Rafael Rodríguez, chief economist, planner, and former member of the PSP who is in charge of foreign relations. The prime minister seems to have turned his energies outside of the country. From the end of 1971 to the end of 1973, he spent a total of four months travelling abroad. Through an intergovernmental Cuban-Soviet Commission, controlled from the Cuban side by Rodríguez, the U.S.S.R. has institutionalized its supervision over the use of its economic and military aid to the island. A new wave of Soviet technicians has flooded into Cuba, and native personnel in charge of plants built with Soviet aid are being trained in the U.S.S.R. The Cuban economy and its planning have become even more integrated into the Soviet bloc through the former's entrance into Comecon (or CMEA: Council for Mutual Economic Assistance). Numerous agreements and joint communiqués have been signed by the two countries concerning trade, technical aid, repayment of debts, credits, planning, satellite communication, and foreign policy.

In December 1970, Carlos Rafael Rodríguez led a Cuban delegation to Moscow where meetings were held with a team of Soviet economists headed by Nikolai Baibakov, director of the Soviet Central Planning Board (GOSPLAN). As a result of such conversations, the Cuban-Soviet Commission of Economic, Scientific, and Technical Collaboration was established. In February 1971, the Cuban-Soviet long-term trade and payments agreement for 1965–1970 was temporarily extended until 1975.[5] The signing of a permanent trade agreement was delayed until the Commission had carefully studied the situation. To complete the basic details for the Commission's organization, Baibakov visited Cuba in April and May, and Cuban chancellor Raúl Roa went to Moscow in June 1971. Roa's delegation, which included the President of the Central Bank and the Minister of Foreign Trade, met with Brezhnev, Kosygin, and Gromyko.[6]

The first meeting of the Commission was held in Havana early in September 1971. The Soviet delegation was led by the vice president of the U.S.S.R. Council of Ministers, Vladimir Novikov, and was composed of top officials from the ministries of foreign trade, merchant marine, construction of agricultural and industrial machinery, electricity and civil aviation, as well as the Soviet ambassador in Havana. The Cuban delegation was led by Rodríguez, who also presided over the meetings, and was composed of top officials from the Central Planning Board (JUCEPLAN), the ministries of foreign trade, merchant marine, basic industry, mining-fuel-metallurgy, the state agencies of agricultural mechanization and development, fishing, electricity and aviation, and the Cuban ambassador in Moscow. Rodríguez opened the meetings praising the Soviet role in the birth and support of the Cuban Revolution. In the same line, Novikov reported that Soviet-Cuban trade in 1970 had increased by 60 percent over 1966, reaching more than one billion rubles per year (about three million dollars daily); he also stressed the pivotal importance of Soviet oil, steel, and machinery for the island's economy and listed the factories and plants built with Soviet aid as well as the repairs made in seventy-eight sugar mills (more than half of those in existence).[7]

The agenda for the meeting included the establishment of a more efficient system of training the Cuban personnel in charge of the Soviet-made plants; Cuban reports on the measures adopted to make up for the delays caused by the 1970 sugar-harvest mobilization in the Soviet-aid construction of one electrical plant and two fertilizer plants; and the possibility of future Soviet cooperation in mechanizing the sugar harvest, expanding electrical capacity, and establishing a pharmaceutical industry in Cuba. Premier Castro attended the signing of the agreements but, unaccustomedly, did not say a word; in the official picture he was standing behind Rodríguez, who was signing the document. The latter thanked the Soviet delegates "for their efforts in organizing and making more effective use of the aid provided by the U.S.S.R." In the protocol, the Cubans agreed to speed up the operation of loading and unloading Soviet vessels in Cuban ports, to accelerate the work at plants being built with Soviet aid, and to send to the U.S.S.R. the technicians who would direct such plants. The Soviet Union promised to send Cuba a new sugar-cane harvester jointly designed by engineers from both countries (the KTP-1) and to provide technical aid for Cuba's attempt to locally produce its own harvesters ("Libertadora" and "Henderson") on a large scale. Tests to be supervised by Soviet experts would be conducted on both machines during the 1972 harvest. Nothing concrete was agreed upon regarding new electrical and pharmaceutical plants.[8] Upon his return to Moscow, Novikov announced that the Commission had also reviewed the fulfillment of trade agreements in 1969–1971.[9]

At the end of October 1971, Premier Alexei Kosygin visited Cuba. He had previously been in Havana in June 1967, on his return to Moscow from his Glassboro meeting with President Johnson. This was at a time when Soviet-Cuban relations were deteriorating, and the important dignitary received a cool official reception and little attention from the Cuban press. In contrast, his second visit was heralded with great fanfare, newspapers devoted almost entire issues to reporting the event, and Kosygin held talks with both Castro brothers, President Dorticós and, of course, Rodríguez. More cordial relations were evident when in a meeting with Castro the Soviet premier said: "We have lost no time in getting together with comrade Fidel. . . . It isn't only on this meeting but also in other matters that we came to a quick understanding with him." Castro replied: "One way to express our gratitude to the U.S.S.R. for their great aid is to extract the maximum out of the Soviet equipment, to use it efficiently, and to keep it in running condition."[10] There was a communiqué signed by both premiers stressing the "complete mutual understanding" reached on the strengthening of politico-economic links between the two nations. In the document, Castro fully endorsed Soviet foreign policy while Kosygin condemned the United States' "illegal holding" of the Guantánamo base and invited Castro to visit the U.S.S.R.[11]

In November 1971, Castro partly accepted responsibility for Cuba's previous conflicts with the Soviet Union; one month later, in Moscow, Dorticós acknowledged that the U.S.S.R. was the leading socialist country in the world. Once the frictions between the two countries had been overcome, Kosygin announced in Moscow that conversations had begun on the signing of a trade agreement for 1972–1975 that would replace the old 1965–1970 agreement which had been provisionally extended.[12] (In the meantime, the old trade agreement was hurting Cuba economically: in 1972 the international price of sugar was above the 6.11 cents per pound paid to Cuba by the U.S.S.R. In December 1971, the latter paid 7.14 cents per pound for 270,000 tons of sugar bought from Brazil, the archenemy of Cuba.)[13]

The extent to which Cuba had departed from Sino-Guevarism and sided with the Soviets became evident in the treatment given by the Cuban press to Nixon's visit to China and his visits to Moscow and Warsaw in 1972. Reports of Nixon's visit to China were cleverly manipulated by the Cuban press to criticize the Chinese. In one issue of the party newspaper *Granma*, the front page was divided into two halves: the top half contained news and photographs of the U.S. bombing of Vietnam, while the bottom half had photographs of Nixon shaking hands with Mao and Chou En-lai. The newspaper also reproduced excerpts of the friendly toasts exchanged between Nixon and Chou, and its last page was full of well-selected, embarrassing photographs with ironic comments.[14] In contrast, Nixon's visits to Moscow and Warsaw were reported factually (taken from TASS), although very briefly, not in prominent places, and without evaluation or comment.[15]

The second meeting of the Cuban-Soviet Commission was held in Moscow on April 10–15, 1972, but scanty information is available about it. Rodríguez was the head of the Cuban delegation, and Novikov presided over the meeting. The composition of the delegations was similar to that of the first meeting. At this meeting, mechanization of the sugar harvest was discussed, and the results of the tests done during the 1972 sugar crop on the various types of cane-harvesters were probably evaluated. (Significantly, in June, the U.S.S.R. announced that a factory to build the KPT-1 model—sponsored by the Soviets—would be sent to Cuba.) The Commission also agreed to supply Cuba with an electronic computer to help in economic planning, thus strengthening Rodríguez's position in favor of a more technical and powerful central planning apparatus. (At the same time that the Commission was holding its sessions, representatives of the central planning boards of both countries, the Soviet GOSPLAN and the Cuban JUCEPLAN, were discussing collaboration in planning.) Other topics discussed were the mechanization and modernization of ports (the inefficiency of loading and unloading Soviet ships had been a matter of discussion in the first meeting), civil aviation, irrigation, hydroelectric energy, a pharmaceutical industry, education, and communications. Rodríguez decorated Novikov with the medal of the Cuban Academy of Sciences, met with Kosygin, and travelled to Berlin.[16]

Although the subject of military aid was not included in either of the two agreements of the Commission, events in 1972 showed that this was on the agenda. Early in January the Cuban Navy received several Soviet missile-carrying launches that doubled its missile and anti-aircraft equipment.[17] In April, the air force, in turn, received a flotilla of MIG-23s, the most technologically advanced Soviet aircraft, which modernized the Cuban stock of MIG-15s, MIG-17s, MIG-19s, and MIG-21s. For several months a team consisting of hundreds of Soviet military experts led by Lt. General Dimitri Krutskikn had been training Cuban personnel in the use of this equipment. The ceremony to present the airplanes received wide publicity; it was opened by Krutskikn, who was followed by the Soviet ambassador in Cuba, Nikita Tulubeev, and it was closed by Minister of the Armed Forces Raúl Castro, who said that the military aid was proof of Soviet confidence.[18]

In May 1972, Castro began a trip to Africa and Eastern Europe, which lasted sixty-three days (May 2-July 6), longer than all of his previous trips abroad put together. Before taking off, the premier said: "Only a few years ago none of us would even dream of being outside of our country for too long, considering the way the imperialists were acting, with all their threats. Fortunately things are different now."[19] Castro was no longer afraid of the possibility of an invasion, either directly by or sponsored by the United States. He was concerned, however, about the Soviet commitment to détente with the United States, which was manifested by the fact that Nixon's decision to blockade North Vietnamese ports and escalate the bombing of the North did not impede his visit to Moscow. Probably the announcement of this visit precipitated Castro's trip to Eastern Europe. In Castro's mind, Cuba and Vietnam were in a similar position; thus, he devoted a large portion of his speeches in Eastern Europe to attacking the United States and pledging solidarity with the Vietnamese. In his speech on arriving in Poland—Nixon had just left—Castro pointed out that Cuba was not part of any security pact or military alliance (an obvious reference to the Warsaw Pact) but depended only on its own power. He was evidently attempting to apply pressure on the Soviets before his arrival in Moscow.

Brezhnev rhetorically responded to this strategy by condemning the U.S. blockade and bombing of North Vietnam as well as the U.S. occupation of the Guantánamo base in Cuba. He assured Castro that the policy of peaceful coexistence would not weaken the ideological struggle, that the confrontation between capitalism and communism would become more acute rather than weaker, and that small socialist nations would be defended and treated equally by the Soviet superpower. Apparently satisfied, Castro said that for twelve years the United States had exerted pressure on Cuba to break its ties with the U.S.S.R. but that, instead, the relations between the two countries had consolidated, reaching a level never attained before, and that Cuban confidence in the U.S.S.R. had been strengthened. Then he pledged that Cuba would never accept "opportunism, neutralism, revisionism, liberalism, or capitalist ideological penetration." One wonders whether this statement was a betrayal of his subconscious hope that the Soviet Union would abstain from such vicious practices.

In addition to showing his concern about the Soviet rapprochement with the United States, Castro's trip also made evident his new, more compromising attitude toward other countries. Four or five years earlier when Houari Boumédienne overthrew Ben Bella, who had supported Castro and whom Castro had supported, the Cuban press was strongly critical of Boumédienne. However, Castro began his long trip with a stay in Algeria of nine days, equal to the time he later spent in the U.S.S.R. (The nine days in Algeria were followed by six days in revolutionary Guinea and one day in traditional Sierra Leone.) Castro had also earlier sorted friend from foe by the country's prevailing antagonism toward the U.S.S.R.; hence, Rumania had been very high in his esteem several years ago. Now the length of stay in each of the Eastern European countries was positively correlated to their orthodoxy and good standing with Moscow: nine days in the U.S.S.R., eight in East Germany and

Bulgaria, seven in Poland and Hungary, five in Czechoslovakia, and four in Rumania.

Rodríguez joined Castro for the Eastern European stage of his trip, replacing Major Juan Almeida, a black who had been an asset during the African stage of the trip. (Some members of the Cuban delegation who were ideologically unacceptable to the U.S.S.R. also returned to Havana.) Both the Cuban and the Eastern European news media ranked Rodríguez second in the Cuban delegation. He was decorated in several countries and in the Moscow meetings he, Castro, Brezhnev, Kosygin, and Podgorny met alone. Photographs of Rodríguez at important meetings were frequently shown; he apparently was taking care of the serious business. During the trip, Castro did all that he could to build up his own image. He submitted to unaccustomed formalities such as wearing a necktie to receive the Dimitrov Order in Bulgaria and the Lenin Order in Moscow, and wearing a cap and gown in his investment as Doctor Honoris Cause at Charles University in Prague. On the other hand, he played his old role of a populist, charismatic leader, visiting dozens of factories and farms even in remote areas, playing football with Bulgarians and basketball with Poles, and often mixing with the population. Castro's visit to the U.S.S.R. was originally scheduled for three weeks but lasted only nine days. When leaving the country, the prime minister said that he would return in 1973 or 1974 "for a more extended unofficial visit." Rodríguez stayed in Moscow for a few days after Castro left, preparing a significant announcement.

On July 11, 1972, at Comecon's twenty-sixth meeting, Rodríguez officially requested Cuba's entrance into the organization, and its eight members unanimously accepted.[20] Rodríguez promised to eliminate "once and for all" the instability of the Cuban supply of sugar to the socialist camp, asked Comecon's support in developing Cuba's nickel industry and derivates of sugar-cane bagasse, and requested entry into the Intergovernmental Commission of Socialist Countries for the Development of Electronic Computation. In turn, Kosygin stated that the needs of the Cuban economy should be coordinated with the 1976–1980 plans of Comecon members.[21]

In the West, there was the impression before Castro's trip that neither he nor the Soviet leaders were eager for Cuba's entrance into

Comecon.[22] After the step was taken, it was speculated that Cuba's admission could be a Soviet concession to give guarantees to Castro that Moscow's improved ties with Washington would not be detrimental to the remote Caribbean island.[23] But if this was the case and Castro had a vested interest in getting such a "concession," why did he not stay in Moscow for five more days to make the request himself? What he probably wanted was Cuba's admittance into the Warsaw Pact, but this was too much to ask of the Soviets because it might have jeopardized their delicate new détente with the United States. It is doubtful that Cuba's entrance into Comecon would bring any significant advantage to the island; and, conversely, it may result in less flexibility in Cuban economic plans, now to be coordinated with those of the seven Eastern European nations (and Mongolia!). This step will personally reduce Castro's power in economics even more and strengthen that of Rodríguez. On the other hand, it may be advantageous to the U.S.S.R. Since it dominates Comecon, the U.S.S.R. may try to distribute the Cuban economic burden more equally among Comecon members. The Soviets also hope that through more "scientific and sound economic collaboration" Cuba will fulfill its sugar supply commitments with Comecon members. Soviet sugar output is ten million tons, enough to satisfy domestic consumption and export commitments with some Comecon members. But production of the Soviet sugar beet is very costly, and it would be more efficient to use this land for other crops with higher yield and value. Thus if Cuba is capable of becoming the steady supplier of sugar to Comecon, the U.S.S.R. would be able to cut its sugar output and exports. Furthermore, the Soviets would be able to fully utilize their sugar refineries increasing their productivity by refining Cuban sugar. The Soviet sugar harvest takes place during a different season than Cuba's and hence their refineries would be operating most of the year.[24]

Cuban dependence on the U.S.S.R. seemed to have reached a point of no return in 1972. Some 60 percent of Cuban trade was with the Soviets (70 percent with Comecon), approximately the same proportion it had been with the United States in the 1950s.[25] Cuba had also systematically failed to meet its sugar export commitments with the Soviets, thereby building in 1965–1972 a cumulative deficit of 20 million tons of sugar, the equivalent of three good sugar crops.[26] According to Soviet sources, the island's cumulative trade deficit with the U.S.S.R. for 1960–1970 amounted to $1.5 billion; but Cuban statistics for the same period gave a figure above $2 billion.[27] Due to the bad sugar crops of 1971–1972 (and a bad tobacco crop in 1971), Cuba's cumulative trade deficit with the U.S.S.R. may have increased to $3 billion by 1972.[28] Cuba's total debt to the Soviet Union in 1972 was probably close to $4 billion if the annual repayment of loans ($130–150 million) plus interest, shipping costs, and the cost of maintaining Soviet technical and military advisors were added. It has been reported that the National Bank of Cuba estimates that half of this debt could have been saved if Cuba traded with market economies.[29] Cuba's merchant marine, despite its remarkable growth in the last decade, carried only 7–8 percent of the island trade, most of which was handled by Soviet vessels.[30] The U.S.S.R. gave Cuba $1.5 billion in military aid until 1971; and although apparently not charging for it, the U.S.S.R. has gained substantial control in the supervision of such equipment. Diplomatic sources in Havana conservatively estimated that in the summer of 1971 there were some 3,000 Soviet technicians and military advisors in Cuba.[31] Some 1,500 Cubans who will be in key positions (85 percent of them engineers and technicians) were being trained in the U.S.S.R. in 1973, a number similar to all the Cubans that studied there in 1961–1971.[32]

In the 1960s, conflicts between the U.S.S.R. and Cuba were generated by several causes. Cuba often felt treated in a neo-colonial manner by a big power. The first serious crisis between the two nations occurred in 1962 when the Soviet Union agreed with the United States (without consulting Cuba) to withdraw the missiles that had created the October crisis. Six years later, Castro accused the "developed socialist countries" of using commercial practices similar to those employed by the capitalist countries and specifically denounced the U.S.S.R. for restricting its oil supplies to Cuba, thus obstructing the latter's development. Other points of friction resulted from divergent doctrinal stands; thus, in 1966–1968 (the Sino-Guevarist stage) Castro imputed the Soviets with neglecting ideological consciousness and political awareness for the development of the material base and with introducing economic reforms that pushed them back to capitalism.[33]

In his speech of July 26, 1972, the Cuban prime minister showed how his dependence on the Soviets had forced him to retreat from his previous critical positions. He said that Cuban-Soviet relations were "based on principles and doctrine" and that "the success of the Revolution [and] its principled policy" had been made possible and was guaranteed by the U.S.S.R. He reported that since his 1964 visit to the U.S.S.R. impressive Soviet progress had occurred in technology, economics, science, and in the cities, and stated that this development of the material base had been paralleled by the achievement of a "tremendous political awareness": "It is an unquestionable fact that imperialist ideology, propaganda and corruption have not succeeded in gaining a toehold anywhere in the Soviet Union. . . . Marxism-Leninism lives on there, [it] is the daily bread of the Soviet people." Finally Castro stated that the Soviet leadership had "deep feelings of solidarity, affection, and respect" for the Cuban people and that they, in turn, were "proud to have the priceless, disinterested, and revolutionary" friendship of the U.S.S.R.: "The economic relations between Cuba and the Soviet Union have been the most generous and the most revolutionary possible. . . . Relations of this kind used to be unknown in the history of relations among nations. . . . Though the world of tomorrow will change, our friendship with the Soviet people will remain a constant and our gratitude will be eternal."[34]

In November 1972, there was an important reorganization of the top Cuban government apparatus: an Executive Committee with power above the Council of Ministers was established, composed of ten deputy prime ministers with direct control over sectors of the economy and administration, each one grouping several central ministries and agencies. Castro became the president of the New Executive Committee and retained the premiership of the Council of Ministries and his control over several ministries and agencies, principally the armed forces and internal security. But, obviously, there was some delegation of his previous omnipotence. Rodríguez was appointed deputy minister of foreign policy with control over the Cuban-Soviet Commission and foreign relations. President Dorticós was given control over JUCEPLAN, the Ministries of Foreign Trade and Labor, the National Bank, and other minor agencies.[35] Nevertheless, Rodríguez's control over the foreign sector gives him enormous power in foreign trade (in addition, this ministry is headed by Marcelo Fernández, a follower of Rodríguez's economic thought) and his expertise on planning a *de facto* control over JUCEPLAN.

The Cuban-Soviet Commission, Cuba's entrance into Comecon, the strengthening of the former's planning apparatus, and the increasing influence of Rodríguez and other technocrats trusted by the U.S.S.R. assured the latter that the island would use Soviet aid more efficiently, follow a more conventional and rational economic policy, and do its best to honor its export commitments in the future. And yet Cuba's accumulated debt was so colossal that it jeopardized the new economic strategy. Important concessions were necessary to allow such a strategy to consolidate, bear fruit, and eradicate the negative image of Cuba's poor economic performance which had been so embarrassing for the Soviets all over the world, particularly in Latin America.

In December 1972, Castro and Rodríguez returned to Moscow to participate in the festivities surrounding the fiftieth anniversary of the founding of the U.S.S.R. As part of the celebrations a plenary meeting of all the participants was held; Castro, in a final political concession, proposed at this meeting that the Soviet "single multinational state" become a model for a "Latin American socialist community."[36] The next day he and Brezhnev signed five economic agreements through which the U.S.S.R. made the following important commitments: 1) a stipulation for higher prices in 1973–1975 for Cuba's two main export items—sugar (an increase from 6.11 to 11 cents per pound) and nickel; 2) technical aid in 1973–1975 (at a value of 300 million rubles) to mechanize the sugar harvest, to repair, modernize and/or expand nickel, electricity, oil-refining, textile, and metallurgic installations, and to help in planning and electronic computation (this credit will be paid in 1976–2000); 3) deferment for thirteen years of the payment of the Cuban debt to the U.S.S.R. (both principal and interest) accrued in 1960–1972 (payments will be made in 1986–2011); 4) granting of the necessary credit to compensate for the expected Cuban deficit in the balance of payments in 1973–1975 with the Soviets (probably about one billion rubles) under the same payment conditions as in the third commitment above; and, 5) a three-year (1973–1975) trade agreement (details were not given).[37] The numerous concessions made by Cuba since 1970 had finally paid off economically, but the island's dependency on the U.S.S.R. was greater than ever before and extended into the twenty-first century.

The third meeting of the Cuban-Soviet Commission was held in Havana from February to March 1973, to implement the new economic agreements signed in Moscow. Rodríguez, the head of the meeting, opened it with praise of the U.S.S.R. for the concessions made.[38] After the meeting was over, two significant events took place. On March 13, 1973, Rodríguez gave the closing speech of the act commemorating the sixteenth anniversary of the attack on the Presidential Palace by the Student Directorate.[39] This speech had been traditionally pronounced by Fidel Castro or a representative of the Student Directorate. The assignment of the speech to Rodríguez was a symbolic "cleaning" of responsibility of the PSP. In 1964 several members of the PSP had been accused by Castroites of revealing to Batista's police the hiding place of various members of the Directorate who had attacked the Palace in 1957 resulting in their deaths at the hands of the police.[40] In April 1973, Joaquín Ordoqui, one of the former PSP members who was involved in the accusation and held in home confinement since 1964, was freed without being brought to trial because "his collaboration had not been established." These were two significant political concessions granted by Castro to the U.S.S.R., probably in reciprocity for the economic agreements.

Cuba's relations with Eastern Europe were strengthened even more in 1973 with official visits of important dignitaries from the latter to the former. In April, Gustav Husak, first secretary general of the Czechoslovak Communist party heard Castro praise his country for being the first to send weapons to Cuba in the early 1960s and for the numerous factories sold to the island.[41] This was a significant rectification of Castro's accusations at the time of the Soviet invasion of Czechoslovakia in the sense that the latter had sold obsolete weapons and factories to Cuba.[42] In May, it was the Poles' turn: Henryk Jablonsky, chairman of the Council of State, and Wojciech Jaruzelski, minister of defense. In June, Castro accepted an invitation, made by an official delegation of the League of Communists of Yugoslavia touring Cuba, to visit Yugoslavia.[43] This would have been inconceivable five years before when that party had been publicly denounced by Castro as an imperialist agent and Titoism as a rightist tendency.[44] In August, Nicolae Ceausescu, general secretary of the party and chairman of the State Council of Rumania, visited Cuba and granted it a $65 million loan for a new cement factory.

In September 1973, Castro attended the Fourth Conference of Nonaligned Nations in Algiers. His trip took more than two weeks because the Cuban prime minister paid short visits to Guyana, Trinidad and Tobago, Guinea, Baghdad, New Delhi, Prague, Hanoi, and the areas controlled by the RSV in South Vietnam.[45] In his speech at the Algiers conference, Castro rejected the theory of "two imperialisms" (the United States and the U.S.S.R.) "encouraged by theoreticians from the capitalist world and echoed by leaders of nonaligned countries" who hence had "betrayed the cause of internationalism from supposedly revolutionary positions." He reminded the audience of the "glorious, heroic, and extraordinary services rendered to the human race" by the U.S.S.R. and labeled as counterrevolutionary any criticism against it: "Inventing a false enemy [the U.S.S.R.] can have only one aim, to evade the real enemy [the United States]."[46] This speech created a split in the conference, provoked an irate interruption by Cambodia's Prince Norodom Sihanouk, and a strong attack by Libya's President Muammar el-Qaddafi who said: "We are against Cuba's presence in this Conference of Nonaligned Nations. There is no difference between Cuba and any East European country, or for that matter Uzbekistan and the Soviet Union itself."[47] Reportedly the affair upset Houari Boumédienne, the host of the conference, and precipitated the Cuban break in relations with Israel to please the Arab nations. The Cuban press only gave coverage to Castro's interventions, disregarded the incidents in the conference, and neither published Boumédienne's speech nor the conclusions of the conference. Scarcely one year after the economic agreements were signed in Moscow, they were producing an excellent political payoff: Castro had not only become "safe" but was the staunchest, most unconditional defender of the U.S.S.R. both at home and abroad. This series of events was to culminate in 1974 with Brezhnev's visit to Cuba.

The visit of the Secretary of the Soviet Communist Party had been a matter of long negotiation. In his trips to the U.S.S.R. in July and December of 1972, Castro had personally invited Brezhnev to visit Cuba. In June 1973, when the Soviet leader met Nixon in the United States, the Cubans hoped that Brezhnev would stop in Havana on his way back to Moscow. But he did not, concerned that such a visit could have been seen by the United States as an unfriendly gesture. Instead he announced, upon his return to Moscow, that he had accepted Castro's invitation to visit Cuba by the end of the year. Early in December, Rodríguez went to Moscow to discuss the travel plans but the Soviet leader—probably worried that his presence in the festivities of the fifteenth anniversary of the Revolution in Havana would embarrass the United States—postponed the trip again, this time until the end of January.[48] Still cautious, Brezhnev addressed greetings to President Nixon from aboard the plane carrying him to Cuba, only one hour from Havana, and said: "I am confident that relations between the Soviet Union and the United States will be developing further to the benefit of the peoples of our two countries and in the interest of international security and universal peace."[49]

Cuba prepared a great reception for the first visit of Brezhnev to a Latin American country and "the most important ever" in Cuban history. A week before the trip, the Cuban media gave wide biographical coverage to Brezhnev. The day of his arrival the newspaper *Granma* devoted the whole first page to a closeup of the Soviet dignitary, topped by "welcome" in Russian. Cuban and Soviet flags adorned Havana, the Ministry of Labor declared a national holiday, the traffic routing in Havana was modified to facilitate the visit, and the Cubans shouted words of welcome in Russian. The population was exhorted to attend a mass rally after the airport reception and maps were published to that effect.[50] Brezhnev's arrival, the airport reception, and the mass rally were transmitted live and in color to an estimated 170 million viewers in the U.S.S.R.[51] One million Cubans gathered in the mass rally for what was considered "the most grandiose, gigantic, and extraordinary ever held in the nation."

In his welcoming speech at the rally, Castro reviewed fifteen years of revolution and the role played in it by the United States. He made an important concession by acknowledging for the first time that in the 1962 Missile Crisis the U.S.S.R. played a crucial role in avoiding Cuba's invasion by U.S. forces and guaranteeing the security of the island. In spite of his criticism of the United States, Castro indirectly supported the Soviet-U.S. détente to reduce international tension and stop the arms race. The Cuban prime minister ended his speech defending the Soviet Union from attacks of "pseudo leftists" and promised: "We will never be disloyal or ungrateful to the U.S.S.R."[52] Brezhnev opened his speech praising the Cubans for having "reached a stage of development" in which they were building the foundations of socialism "in a positive and systematic manner." The thrust of the speech was peaceful coexistence. He stated that the normalization of Soviet-American relations was an indisputable step forward in achieving world peace and that they would continue in that path. Referring to Latin America, Brezhnev said: "The Soviet Union considers inadmissible and criminal any attempt to export the counterrevolution. . . . By the same token we Communists are not partisans of the exportation of the revolution. This should ripen in the soil of each country. How and when it emerges, what forms and methods it uses is only the business of the people in each country." As if this had not been sufficiently clear to the Cubans, he ended the speech saying: "Soviet weapons in Cuban hands are neither to attack anybody nor a tool to aggravate international tension. They serve to the fair cause of the [domestic Cuban] defense."[53]

In the Cuban-Soviet communiqué signed by Brezhnev and Castro at the end of the visit, both countries declared a "total unity" in their ideas and positions in world affairs, in favor of cohesion of the international communist movement, and against any attempt to split it (an indirect reference to China). They also condemned revisionism from either the right or the left, renounced the use of force, and agreed that the normalization of Soviet-American relations was an important step towards world peace.[54] Brezhnev's visit consolidated the new stage of the Cuban Revolution and showed how Soviet influence had contributed to shape that stage.

Idealism Bows to Pragmatism

In Sino-Guevarist thought, "subjective conditions" (ideas, consciousness, willingness; all belonging to the superstructure in Marxist terms) can decisively influence "objective conditions," that is, the material base, the forces of production, the structure which in the orthodox interpretation of Marxism determines the superstructure. (Thus a socialist revolution took place in Cuba, although the material base was not ripe for it, because of the consciousness of the guerrilla *foco*.) The successful development of consciousness (ahead of the material-base development) can enable a country to skip the transitional stage of development between capitalism and communism (i.e., socialism) or, as the Cubans put it, to build socialism and communism simultaneously. The U.S.S.R. rejects this interpretation of Marxism, arguing that a socialist country cannot go further than the development of its material base allows it to. Here lies the Soviet emphasis on building the material base first. Soviet ideologists have transformed the original two-step development ladder into four: "building the foundations of socialism," "full socialism," "building the foundations of communism," and "full communism," and placed the U.S.S.R. at the third step as the most advanced country in the socialist world.

In August 1970, Castro announced: "The Revolution is now entering a new phase; a much more serious, mature, profound phase."[55] He explained that at the beginning of the Revolution there were many people who thought that its triumph "was the result of some sort of magic," and others who minimized the difficulties faced by the revolutionary government, alleging that these difficulties "could be whisked away very easily." In order to be successful, Castro warned, the Cuban had to be carefully realistic in the future:

Let's not do as we have done so often, when we get an idea . . .

putting it into practice without further ado, only to discredit
the idea later because . . . it was taken directly from the brain
to the world of reality where it died for lack of minimal
[objective] conditions. . . . Some [unrealistic theorists] try to
impose their ideas on reality rather than reality on their
ideas.[56]

In September, Castro put in doubt the possibility of skipping or
accelerating the stages of development: "Perhaps our major idealism
has been to believe that a society which has scarcely left the shell of
capitalism could enter, in one bound, into a society in which
everyone would behave in an ethical and moral manner."[57] Three
months later, he recommended going "slowly to arrive quickly;
slowly to arrive well; and slowly to be sure to arrive!"[58] On May Day
1971, the premier stated:

> The way to communism is not a question of consciousness
> alone. It also has to do with the development of the forces of
> production. . . . We cannot fall into the idealism of thinking
> that . . . consciousness has been developed and that we already
> have the necessary material base. . . . This really is not the
> case . . . ["our consciousness has a long way to go in the matter
> of development"]. . . . We must understand that we are in a
> transitional stage . . . that we cannot just act as if we were
> already in communism. . . . If in the pursuit of communism
> we idealistically go further ahead than is possible, we will have
> to retreat sooner or later.[59]

During his visit to Chile in November 1971, he sadly acknowledged:
"Let us not forget one thing, and that is that spontaneity does not
solve any problems. . . . It is easier to change the structure than to
change the conscientiousness of man." Answering a newspaperman
who asked him whether there were contradictions in the relations
between Cuba and the socialist countries, he said: "We have had
contradictions at times. On occasion those contradictions were due to
a certain idealism [from our side] . . . we expected things to develop
the way our imagination pictured them."[60]

At the end of 1971, the Cuban newspaper *Granma* reported on its front page that in a meeting held in Moscow between Secretary General Brezhnev and visiting Cuban president Dorticós, the latter spoke of the efforts aimed at "creating the foundations of socialism" in Cuba while the former reported on "the progress made in the construction of communism" in the U.S.S.R.[61] Thus Cuba acknowledged being at the bottom of the Soviet-invented, four-step ladder to full communism, two steps below its protectors. Dorticós also expressed his gratitude "for the public recognition by the Soviet Union of the significance of the Cuban Revolution with respect to the liberation movements in Latin America." This subservient attitude would have been inconceivable during the 1960s when the Cubans attempted to lead the Third-World revolutionary movement, thus challenging the Soviets. The new mood was for coexistence and moderation; hence, in another meeting, Kosygin warmly welcomed the increasing number of Latin American states in favor of reestablishing commercial and diplomatic relations with Cuba.

In November 1972, Carlos Rafael Rodríguez in his official speech commemorating the fifty-fifth anniversary of the Bolshevik Revolution, made a clever manipulation of Cuban history to adapt it to the current circumstances. First he pointed out that Guevara, at the beginning of the Revolution, was a great admirer of the U.S.S.R. recalling that when Che visited Moscow in 1960 he was "deeply impressed" not only with the great material transformation that was going on there but also with the "Soviet man," the one who was going to create the communist society. Second, Rodríguez quoted Castro during his 1972 visit to the U.S.S.R. when the latter praised the impressive development of the Soviet material base and said that it had been paralleled by an increase in the degree of awareness of the Soviet man in the ideological field, political culture, and revolutionary firmness and asserted that there were no traces of "ideological penetration" by capitalism in the U.S.S.R. Rodríguez then reached the corollary (skipping almost a decade of Cuban history, from 1962 to 1970) that Castro, together with the PCC, had "carried out throughout the Cuban Revolution" Marxism-Leninism as interpreted by the Soviets.[62]

Materials being used in the 1972–1973 "Course on Political Education" taken by party members criticized idealism and spontaneous development of social consciousness as unscientific while giving full support to the Soviet standard interpretation that the mode of production (or material base) is the generator of social consciousness and never vice versa.[63]

In his 1973 speech commemorating the twentieth anniversary of the attack on the Moncada Barracks, the beginning of his Revolution, Fidel Castro stated: "Marx said that rights can never be more advanced than the economic structure and the cultural [consciousness] development determined by it." He then accepted that in the current stage of Cuban development distribution should not be done according to needs but according to work and that excessive use of moral incentives would lead to idealism. He concluded: "If we think and act as if [the attitude of the minority of conscious leaders] was the conduct of every member of society, we would be guilty of idealism and the results would be negative on the economy."[64] Insisting on the same topic, Castro said a few months later:

> In certain cases we tried to make more headway than we were prepared for . . . if you try to go farther than you can, you are forced to retreat. . . . A series of measures and principles of a certain communist character have been put into effect since the triumph of the Revolution. . . . There are many examples to show us we are not yet prepared to live in communism. . . . We should have the courage to correct idealistic mistakes we have made [in the past].[65]

While the painful denunciation of past idealism and the acceptance of reality was being manifested, the Cubans were reintroducing the post-reform Soviet system in the island, slowly, prudently, and without fanfare.

2

Economics:
Realism and Rationality

The revolutionary economic policy of the second half of the 1960s gave predominance to the development of the "New Man" while ignoring many basic economic laws. Such policy was characterized by extreme idealism, labor mobilization, egalitarianism, moral incentives, and gigantic sugar production harvests while negligent of central planning, capital and labor productivity, and financial stability. The failure to reach the grandiose targets, the economic dislocation of 1970, and the increasing Soviet pressure for economic rationalization were the main determinants in the policy shift. The new, pragmatic economic policy, more conventional by Soviet standards, emphasizes central planning and computer development, efficient allocation and use of capital, labor productivity, reduction in the financial disequilibrium ("socialist inflation"), material incentives, and a more balanced economy with less emphasis on sugar. The economic results of this policy are positive in terms of industrial output, overall economic growth, and increased consumer satisfaction. Conversely, such policy may induce selfishness, some stratification, and unemployment pockets. The goal of the "New Man" in an egalitarian and mobilized society has been postponed, but for the man in the street this pragmatic decision probably does not look too bad after all.

Strengthening the Planning Apparatus

In the Cuban debate of 1963–1965, both sides advocated a rational, efficient, centralized planning system with the use of mathematical techniques and computers but with one significant difference: Guevara dreamed of a perfect plant that would completely replace market mechanisms—the cybernetic solution supported in the U.S.S.R. by the conservative politicians and old-style planners. Conversely, Rodríguez, more pragmatic and knowledgeable, sponsored centralized planning with the limited aid of market mechanisms—following the timid economic reform introduced in the U.S.S.R. in 1962–1965. Castro did not buy either of the two variants. In 1966 he drastically reduced the power and functions of the Central Planning Board (JUCEPLAN), discarded the medium-range plan (only partially tried in 1962–1965), probably discontinued the annual plans (in 1965–1970), assumed a number of the decisions formerly made by the planners, seriously neglected computation and statistical gathering, and launched a series of "mini," "extra," or "special" plans. These plans, designed to tackle a particular aspect of the economy, received priority and were entrusted to loyal *fidelistas* who had to report only to the prime minister. Frequently, capital and human resources were transferred from a project in operation (which was left uncompleted or badly functioning) to start new "mini" plans, which in many cases ended in failure.[1]

In 1965 Rodríguez was removed by Castro from his job as president of the National Institute of Agrarian Reform (INRA) and given a ministry "without portfolio." Displaced from one of the most important centers of economic activity, Rodríguez put all his energies into planning research. He organized a team of eleven statisticians and economists, which by 1968 had computerized the first (although rudimentary and incomplete) input-output table of the industrial sector of the Cuban economy. When Leontief, the inventor of input-output, visited Cuba in 1969, he was impressed by the expertise of Rodríguez's team and reported that it had moved its headquarters to JUCEPLAN.[2]

In 1970 when the new stage of the Revolution began, Rodríguez combined two key attributes: he headed Cuba's leading team of experts on central planning and computer techniques and—being a former member of the prerevolutionary PSP—had the confidence of the Soviets. The desperate internal need for economic rationalization and Soviet pressure for a technical approach in planning pushed Rodríguez back to the fore. In a rapid sequence of successes, he became the founder and chairman (on the Cuban side) of the Cuban-Soviet Commission of Economic, Scientific and Technical Collaboration; the deputy prime minister of foreign policy; the chief negotiator of foreign-trade agreements; the Cuban delegate to several socialist transnational committees on planning, trade, and electronic computation; and the man with *de facto* control of domestic planning. (President Dorticós, another moderate-pragmatist trusted by the Soviets, is theoretically in charge of economics and planning.)

The acceptance of the Soviet "model" and the rise of the technocrats resulted in two clear changes: "mini" plans were substituted by short- and medium-range central plans, and computation (particularly for application to planning and management) was rapidly developed. (There were also indications that certain market tools were being considered to improve the allocation and use of investment as well as managerial performance—this aspect will be discussed below.)

It seems that the year 1971 was one of transition and preparation for the dramatic changes in planning. Probably in this year, the ground work to improve the system of statistical collection—which had been neglected in 1966–1970—was also done. By the end of the year, JUCEPLAN had published its biannual statistical bulletin (1969–1970) but it left out (as had the 1967–1968 bulletin) the global economic indicators that were discontinued in 1966.[3] By early 1972, JUCEPLAN was preparing a global economic model for 1973–1975.[4] This would encompass the Cuban economy during the last three years of the 1971–1975 plan, already being implemented by Comecon members. In mid-1972 it was reported that annual economic plans for 1973, 1974, and 1975 were being drawn. (This was the first news released on annual plans since 1964.) Nothing further was published on the 1973 plan, but in late 1973 it was reported that the Council of Ministers and the PCC Political Bureau had discussed the 1974 plan. The study for the five-year plan (1976–1980) started in 1972 and its actual preparation began by late 1973.[5] (This is the first Cuban five-year plan, there was a four-year plan—1962–1965—that was discarded in 1964.) The Cuban medium-range plan should be completed by the end of 1974 in order to allow enough time for the necessary coordination with similar plans of other Comecon members.[6]

A Center for National Computation and Applied Mathematics (CEMACC) was functioning in Cuba by the end of 1970 and it seems that substantial resources have been invested in it.[7] In 1972, the U.S.S.R. sent Cuba a gigantic electronic computer and, in 1973, a technical team to aid in the application of electronic computation to the 1973–1975 plans. Cuba has been a member of the Inter-governmental Commission of Socialist Countries for the Development of Electronic Computation since 1972.[8] In the 1970s there has been an impressive development of computer science in Cuba: 15 million pesos were invested in new computers in 1971, 54 computers were operating in 1972, 2 computer centers were established, numerous Cuban specialists were sent to the U.S.S.R. for training, Cuba began manufacturing small digital computers, and a first meeting on computer sciences took place in 1972.[9]

Improving Capital Efficiency

During 1962–1970, Cuba saved, with great sacrifices in consumption, an increasingly large proportion of GNP (as much as 31 percent in 1968) for investment purposes. Part of this accumulated capital did not pay off as expected because, largely through the "mini" plans, it was arbitrarily allocated to projects that failed or were left uncompleted, or it was wasted through inefficiency and lack of proper maintenance. Inefficient use of capital was accentuated in 1966–1970 by the Sino-Guevarist neglect of objective conditions, the setting up of overambitious projects, the emphasis on fixing output targets in physical terms, and the distaste for monetary accounting and cost analysis, on the one hand, and excessive reliance on spontaneity, on the other. President Dorticós has said: "In the late

1960s some people assumed a distorted [*"deformada"*] position disregarding costs as an element of bourgeois economies, as if costs did not play a pivotal role in socialist economies."[10]

The year 1971 was symbolically named the "Year of Productivity," marking a clear departure from previous policies and leading toward a more efficient allocation and use of capital. In November, Castro stated: "Frequently, the desire to accomplish a great deal in a short time led us to gather together a large amount of resources. And the result was that we didn't make the most effective use of them—we squandered them." For instance, some fifty thousand tractors imported since 1959 were used for all sorts of non-productive functions such as driving to baseball games, to the beach, to parties, and to visit relatives and friends. Individuals who became tractor operators overnight did not know how to handle and maintain the equipment properly. The result, Castro said, was that "the former owner of a private business had a tractor and it lasted twenty years, but later, when the ownership of that production center passed to the state, a tractor lasted only two, three, or maybe four years."[11] In terms of years of service, the fifty thousand tractors were reduced to about seven thousand.

One month later, Castro pointed out other investment misuses, partly caused by the dropping of the central plan and the proliferation of mini plans. Imported equipment lay unutilized for years (sometimes rusting on the docks) because the building to house it had not been constructed. A large thermoelectric plant and some factories were nearly completed but could not be put into operation because of a vital missing part. Light cranes broke down as a result of lifting excessively heavy loads. Frequent electric blackouts and water scarcity were caused by neglect of maintenance of electrical installations and the waterpipe system. (In 1971, 120 million cubic yards of water were lost in the city of Havana alone.) Lack of care and maintenance of housing by owner and renters was also common—in the modern housing complex at East of Havana, dwellers took out the toilets and sold them or used doors for firewood.[12] In agriculture, the construction of small dams was not matched by the development of irrigation systems; hence much of the accumulated water could not be used or was wasted. President

Dorticós reported in early 1972 that there was a serious crisis in railroad transportation because out of 300 locomotives only 134 were working, the rest being wrecked by careless workers. He also said that Cuba had the world's highest per capita consumption of spare parts due to poor treatment of equipment. On another occasion Dorticós referred to 145 oil tanks imported from the U.S.S.R. in 1970 which had not been installed by 1972.[13]

The Cuban leadership has announced various measures to correct this situation: future projects will be more realistic according to the nation's level of development; incompleted projects will be finished before new ones are started; maintenance and repair of equipment and adequate training of maintenance personnel will receive priority; quality standards will be strictly enforced in all enterprises; and cost accounting and analysis will be an indispensable tool to increase efficiency.[14] Three concrete measures merit special consideration: training of technical personnel, introduction of a system of economic-data filing, and elaboration of a device to improve the efficiency of investment allocation.

Since late 1970 there has been a revival in Cuba of economic and accounting studies which had suffered a serious setback in 1966–1970. Furthermore, two new careers have been introduced: "systems analyst" and "economic comptroller." The curricula of these careers include mathematical analysis, calculus, statistics, economic theory, planning, systems analysis, informational techniques, accounting, management, and production processes.[15] Graduates are a mixture of accountant, economist, and business administrator. In August 1972, Rodríguez lamented the loss of valuable technicians who fled at the beginning of the Revolution due to excessive radicalism and other errors of the leadership. He promised that currently employed technicians convinced of capitalist advantages but with a "national conscience" would contine to work for the Revolution and acknowledged that the substitution of political cadres for technocrats was an error which led to the failure of the 1970 harvest.[16] One year later President Dorticós warned managers of state enterprises that they had to acquire the necessary qualifications for their jobs or else would be fired regardless of their revolutionary credentials.[17] By the end of 1973, the following stimuli were introduced to raise the technical levels of the labor force: promotion to a higher post must be based on the acquisition of the required skills; enrollment in higher education conveys a right to a paid leave of absence which increases from one to four hours according to the level of study reached; and completion of training is automatically rewarded with a salary increase. There were sanctions too: those who drop out without justification or change their specialization after the training is completed ought to return to the state wages paid during their study leaves.[18]

At the beginning of 1973, the Department of Managerial Analysis of the Center for National Computation (CEMACC) established a system of economic-data filing ("Registro Económico") in the Ministry of Basic Industry and began its gradual expansion to the whole economy (it was expected to be fully operational in 1974). The system maintains a record of the allocation of investment, labor, and inputs to enterprises (both in the "productive" and "non-productive" service sector); measures such inputs in physical and value terms with an attempt to match them; estimates production costs in total and per unit of output; analyzes the efficiency of input utilization; and checks the fulfillment of the planning targets on output, costs, and productivity. Value estimates are made using the current system of prices which the Cubans acknowledge as defective and in need of drastic reform.[19]

The debate on alternative systems of economic organization, lively in 1963–1965 and stopped in 1966–1970, timidly reappeared in 1971 limited to technical and narrow subjects. For example, an article written by a foreign economist criticizing the use of profit as the main indicator of managerial performance in socialist economies (in use in the U.S.S.R. since 1965) was translated in the Cuban official economic journal, *Economía y Desarrollo*. It was followed by a cautious defense of such a system written by a Cuban economist.[20] The discussion is largely concentrated around the question of which is the best technique to evaluate investment alternatives in order to select the most efficient one. A Cuban specialist has said that the old Soviet technique of the "coefficient of relative effectiveness" (practiced in the 1950s and early 1960s) has been superseded in socialist countries by more sophisticated techniques (one of which is the use of the interest rate). However, it seems that the Cubans have a preference for "payoff formulas" based on the time period to return investment instead of the interest-type of technique introduced in the U.S.S.R. in 1965.[21] Thus far the budgetary system of finance appears to prevail but possibly a return to self-financing is taking place already in certain sectors of the economy. In late 1973 two Soviet specialists writing in *Social Sciences*, the official journal of the U.S.S.R., said that in an earlier period (1966–1970) the Cubans had tried to reduce the role of self-financing in the economy: "But reality made necessary to improve management, to use more intensively self-financing and other techniques proper of the socialist stage of development."[22]

Increasing Labor Productivity

A time-loss study conducted in 1968 on more than two hundred enterprises (but not published until mid-1970) revealed that from one-fourth to one-half of the workday was wasted.[23] The causes of this phenomenon were overstaffing of enterprises and the poor enforcement, since 1966 (under the Sino-Guevarist belief in self-consciousness), of the Soviet-style work quota system introduced in Cuba in 1963–1965. Work quotas (or labor norms) assigned to each worker fix how much he should produce in a given time schedule (month, week, day, hour) and are a managerial tool for control of labor productivity.[24]

In July 1970, a newspaperman asked the Minister of Labor whether it was true that work quotas would be reintroduced and if this action was not in contradiction with moral incentives. The minister confirmed the reintroduction of the quotas but avoided the delicate second question, saying that the quotas were indispensable to measure the workers' effort.[25] President Dorticós was more explicit later: "We have lost the levels we had reached on [both] the establishment and control of the labor norms and the technicians on norms who are now working on less important jobs. [In the past] there was excessive confidence placed on spontaneity, in the belief that without labor norms everybody would have worked willingly in an efficient manner . . . We must develop a serious and continuous labor-norm policy and get the technicians back."[26]

From October to November, commissions integrated by managerial personnel, party members, technicians, and skilled workers discussed the reintroduction of the labor norms, which actually began in December. By May 1971, almost 600 enterprises had been normed, and by the end of the year the number had increased to 1,500, including part of the sugar industry. The year 1972 was called the "Year of Emulation," and by May Day more than 3,000 enterprises and 700,000 workers (one-third of state employment) were under the work-quota system. By the end of 1973, some 53,000 enterprises employing 70 percent of all state workers were normed. The plan calls for a technical revision of the norms in 1974.[27]

Other measures taken to increase labor productivity, besides labor norms, are the recently introduced stimuli for workers to raise their skills, mechanization of certain operations, and improvements in labor organization and conditions. A success story that received considerable publicity refers to the reduction of long delays in unloading and loading Soviet merchant vessels in Cuban ports. The average time assigned for this job was eleven days but the longshoremen usually took as many as twenty days (each extra day costing an indemnification to the Cubans). Labor norms were tightened, the U.S.S.R. sent technicians, a new mechanized dock was built in Havana harbor, ship arrivals were coordinated, and job conditions (even using music in the docks!) were greatly improved. The delays were cut by 50 percent in 1972.[28]

The above measures generated in 1972 an overall increase of 21 percent in labor productivity.[29] Such advances, however, were concentrated in industry and in those service activities which are especially important to the economy, but agriculture is still plagued by low labor productivity. In late 1973 Raúl Castro asserted that it was common in state farms that labor costs alone exceeded the value of production. As a significant case, he gave figures from a state farm in which the annual wage bill was $48,000 while the value of output was $8,000, thus resulting in a loss of $40,000 without taking other costs of production into account. Raúl's conclusion was that a large number of workers were unnecessary and that such labor surplus should be eliminated.[30]

In fact, superfluous manpower has been already released mostly in the nonagricultural sector and the government has restricted the hiring of unnecessary workers. In 1971 it was initially estimated that the country needed 300,000 additional workers, but the figure was reduced to only 48,000. Samples taken nationally in 1972 showed that employment had been cut by one percent.[31] According to President Dorticós in mid-1972, although the manpower deficit was still the main problem in the country, there were two provinces (Oriente and Las Villas) in which the opposite was true, resulting in some unemployment.[32] By the end of 1973, Fidel Castro acknowledged that the employment pendulum was swinging the other way and that the manpower deficit was rapidly being filled by a greater demand for jobs: "The time may come when we will have a headache finding jobs for all those who want to work." He promised, however, that solutions would be found to avoid the return of an "army of the unemployed."[33] Apparently, as a first step to cope with the problem, the Confederation of Cuban workers (CTC) requested in its 13th Congress a modification of regulations passed when the manpower deficit was acute. (For a detailed discussion of the Congress, see chapter 3.) Such regulations reserved certain types of service jobs for females to force males into fields in which their physical strength was more necessary. Now that conditions have changed, such service jobs should be reopened to male workers.[34]

Fighting "Socialist Inflation"

Since 1961, there has been spiraling inflation in Cuba generated by a widening gap between the demand for and the supply of consumer goods. Demand rose steadily because the population's disposable income was enlarged by full employment; a guaranteed annual salary for sugar workers even if they did not have work to do in the dead season; the increase in minimum wages and pensions; the expansion of free social services (i.e., education, medical care, social security, burials, public telephone calls, water, sports, and, in part, housing);

and a reduction in the cost of other services (i.e., electricity, gas, and public transportation). Demand for many of these services (e.g., electricity, water, phones) increased additionally due to consumer waste, and use was not controlled because of the free or very cheap supply of such services. On the other hand, the supply of consumer goods was negatively affected by stagnation or the small increase in domestic output, reduction of imports, and exportation of goods that were previously assigned to internal consumption.

In a market economy this disequilibrium would have resulted in a steady increase of prices. Taking an egalitarian approach, the Cuban leadership instead decided to introduce rationing in 1962 and to expand it thereafter to all consumer goods. Most families, however, received a total income that far exceeded the cost of the monthly-ration basket of goods. Excess money in circulation began to grow. In 1970, there were 3,478 million pesos in excess, and the total income of the population exceeded by almost twofold the value of available supply. Hence the population could have lived one year without working.[35] As a result of this situation, the black market (where goods were sold from five to ten times the official price) flourished in spite of government restrictions.[36]

At the end of 1970, Castro said: "Abundance isn't created by decree or law. By decree you can distribute what there is; no decree can distribute what isn't there. [We have to] reduce the money in circulation [otherwise] the black market price will rise."[37] Cigarettes were a good example of this situation. In 1971, 40 percent of the tobacco crop was lost due to drought; but even before this there was a problem in meeting both domestic consumption and export demands for this product. Hence the price of cigarettes in the black market skyrocketed—smokers paid from 12 to 15 pesos per pack, that is, 60 to 75 times the official price. Non-smokers used their cigarette ration to trade for other things in the black market.[38]

In order to reduce the money in circulation, the decision was made to decrease demand and increase supply. To avoid a further increase in demand, the abolition of house rents (scheduled for 1970 and which would have put from 70 to 80 million pesos into circulation) and the raising of bottom wages (promised by Castro in 1968) were postponed indefinitely.[39] Measures to decrease demand included increases in the price of cigarettes, beer, and rum; in rates paid on water and electricity by those who had a high consumption of such utilities; and in the cost of services, such as long-distance transportation and restaurant meals (worker-canteen meals now charge $10 monthly for lunch). In mid-1973, the price of unrationed cigarettes was $2.40 a pack, compared with 20 cents a rationed pack. The price of consumer durables also seemed to have been increased, for instance, $850 for a black and white television set, $550 for a small refrigerator.[40] To cut demand even further, in late 1973, the government reversed some of its previous generous policies. Thus the granting of 100 percent salary to workers in vanguard factories who were sick or retired was eliminated with an estimated annual savings of 140 million pesos. The guaranteed annual wage for sugar workers—which resulted in a subsidy to idle workers during four or five months of the dead season—was being subjected to drastic modification.[41] Cuban decision makers now feel that they were wrong in the 1960s in making public telephone calls and sports shows free and in reducing the price of transportation and cinema tickets but that it will be difficult to reverse such decisions.[42]

Probably the first step to increase the supply of consumer goods was the reduction of the rate of capital accumulation in 1971–1972 to some 28 percent, thus allocating more resources for consumption.[43] In 1972, official sources and foreign press agencies reported that there were more consumer goods available. Although most of the new monthly rations which started in July were unchanged (sugar had been cut from 6 to 4 pounds in February and was cut to 3.5 pounds in December), there was an increase in the butter ration. The supply of fish, milk, some tubers (potatoes, yucca), some fruits (bananas), and both alcoholic and soft beverages was more regular; and there was an apparent increase in the supply of clothing, shoes, and cosmetics. Some 30,000 refrigerators and 250,000 pressure cookers were domestically produced and a large number of non-essential items imported (e.g., transistor radios) or domestically produced (e.g., perfumes, sun glasses). Plans called for 40,000 refrigerators, 100,000 television sets, and 300,000 pressure cookers to be produced in 1973. The government also intended to buy a large number of motorcycles, air conditioners, and cars from

Japan. Restaurants and workers' canteens have improved their menus somewhat, there are plans to build hotels and vacation resorts for workers, and even the carnivals are more sophisticated and luxurious.[44]

The new rationing booklet distributed in the second half of 1973 remained unchanged as far as food was concerned, but introduced significant modifications in manufactured goods. Many of the latter were freed from rationing *("liberados")* and could be bought even when travelling to the interior; among them: film, still and motion-picture cameras, projectors, record players, parts for bicycles and kitchen appliances, coffee sets and crystal cups, silver wedding rings, stationery, plastic shoes and slippers, deodorants, and some cosmetics and perfumes (including brands with such exotic names as "Red Moscow" and "Bulgarian Rose"). A number of goods were put on limited distribution. Two or three times a year each consumer has the option to one or more of the following: toothbrushes, handkerchiefs, socks and stockings, underwear, slacks, pajamas, rubber shoes, raincoats, swim suits, threads, cream cleansers, pots and pans, irons, meat grinders, hoses, and selected furniture. Hotel and vacation resorts were provided with convenient, freed goods such as swim suits, lifesavers, sunglasses, cosmetics, stationery. Some twenty manufactured goods remained strictly rationed such as pants, shirts, dresses, skirts, blouses, leather shoes, fabrics. To facilitate buying each member of the family received a booklet allowing direct purchases, certain goods (such as toys at Christmas time) were to be sold by appointment to avoid long queues, and specialized stores (e.g., for infants) were opened.[45]

As a result of these measures, in the second half of 1971 the amount of money in circulation began to drop. According to Castro, the extraction of money from circulation, in the first quarter of 1972, was due to price increases (13 percent) and to increases in goods and services (87 percent).[46] A total of 1,230 million pesos was taken out of circulation from mid-1971 to the end of 1973: 150 million in 1971, 680 million in 1972, and an estimated 400 million in 1973. The ratio of monetary surplus over total population income was reduced from .87 in 1970 to .47 in 1973. (See table 2.)

By the end of 1973, Castro exclaimed: "Money has started to have

TABLE 2

The Reduction of "Socialist Inflation" in Cuba: 1970-1973
(In millions of pesos)

| | Income | | | | Ratio |
	Total Wage Bill	Other payments to farmers, students, and for pensions	Total (Population Income)	Accumulated Monetary Surplus	M. Surplus over P. Income
1970	3,111	895[a]	4,006[a]	3,478	.87
1971	3,187	948[a]	4,135[a]	3,328	.80
1972	3,367	1,005[a]	4,372[a]	2,648	.61
1973	3,690	1,060	4,750	2,248	.47

[a]Estimates by the author.

Sources: F. Castro, "Discurso en el acto de clausura del XIII Congreso de la CTC," *Juventud Rebelde,* November 16, 1973, pp. 6-7.

some value!"[47] People had less money to spend and hence felt the incentive to work more in order to increase their income and buy the new consumer goods available. This partly explains the increase in the labor supply discussed in the previous section.

Expanding Material Incentives

The apparent rise in the rate of GNP devoted to consumption, the postponement in the granting of new free social services, the partial functioning of market prices, and the increase in the availability of consumer goods are clear indications of a shift away from moral incentives. The excessive emphasis between 1966 and 1970 on moral incentives was not necessarily motivated by ideological reasons but perhaps induced by an excessively high rate of capital accumulation, too much money in circulation, and the acute scarcity of consumer goods. Thus, the sudden stress on wage differentials, a typical material incentive strongly opposed before by the egalitarian trend, is not surprising. Certainly in 1966–1970, under the conditions pointed out above, wage differentials did not make sense as economic stimuli; thus, the emphasis on egalitarianism was logical. In this sense Fidel Castro has said:

> . . . the application of material incentives is useless and ineffective in a situation of tremendous inflation. . . . When everybody has his pockets bulging with money, none of these things [wage differentials, material incentives] is effective. . . . A superabundance of money becomes a disincentive to work for many people.[48]

On May Day 1971, Castro explained that salaries could not be equal for all and that wage differences would be significant in the future as a means of motivating those with labor skills or heavy responsibilities, and those who worked at hard jobs or in places devoid of minimum facilities. If wage differentials were abolished, Castro argued, then those who made an extra effort to acquire skills or had physically hard jobs would be discouraged.[49] The main thesis of the 13th Congress of the CTC was the reinforcement of the socialist system of distribution according to work instead of the communist system of according to need. Castro stated that distribution according to need, as practiced in 1966–1970 could no longer be applied: "Paying the same wage for the same type of work but without taking into account the productive effort required to do it is an egalitarian principle we must correct." Furthermore, the "effort" would not only be measured in physical terms but in the complexity of the job. Hence in 1974, Castro announced, 132 million pesos would be allocated to raise wage rates for technical and managerial personnel to provide a more adequate recompense for their skills. He also announced that cars would be imported to be sold to technicians "in order to increase their productivity."[50]

Other theses approved by the 13th Congress of the CTC dealt with the reintroduction of material incentives (e.g., production bonuses, overtime pay), the elimination of "historical wages," and the new system of socialist emulation.[51] Wages were linked again with the work quotas (as in 1963–1966). If the worker fulfills his quota, he will receive his entire fixed wage; if he doesn't fulfill it, his wage will be reduced in the same proportion of underfulfillment. Finally, if he overfulfills the quota, his wage will be increased proportionally with a bonus. (Not only are bonuses back, but they are paid at a higher proportion than before: 50 percent of overfulfillment in 1963–1966, 100 percent of overfulfillment now).

Overtime pay was massively renounced by the workers in the campaigns of 1968–1970. This is now considered a mistake: "In many cases unpaid overtime turned out to be more costly than regular paid hours of work [because unnecessary overtime was imposed upon the workers who performed poorly while other operating costs were fixed] reducing real production and yield per man hour." The Congress agreed that overtime should be worked only when it is really necessary and then should be paid. Overtime due to the worker's fault should not be paid but entered in his labor record as a "demerit."[52]

"Historical wage" is the difference between the wage that a worker had been assigned prior to the introduction of wage scales in 1963–1965 (and the revision of the 1970s) and the new wage rate assigned to him by the corresponding scale. This addition operates as a disincentive to new workers who joined the labor force after the introduction of the wage-scale system, because they are paid less than workers doing the same job who were hired earlier. The CTC Congress decided to eradicate the "historical wage" through a joint review of each case by the administration and the union. If a worker is found to have the proper skills, he may be offered a higher job; if he doesn't have such skills, an opportunity will be given him for training. If the worker refuses the transfer or retraining, the "historical wage" paid to him will be eliminated.[53]

The new system of socialist emulation approved by the Congress (the fifth in force since 1961) combines material and moral rewards for winners in individual and collectively productive competition. Material rewards for individuals consist of priority to enjoy vacations and recreational programs, and for collectives (e.g., enterprises) to receive allocations for the establishment or improvement of day-care centers and sports and cultural facilities. Moral rewards consist of diplomas, buttons, banners, and honorary titles such as "National Hero of Labor" or "Enterprise of Heroic Effort." Indices to evaluate emulation should be "objective" such as fulfillment of the plan without overtime, cost reductions, proper maintenance, and quality improvements.[54]

The government is making an effort to link the new material incentives closely with workers' productivity. One of the difficulties that moral incentives faced in motivating the workers' efforts was that they were mostly of a communal nature (i.e., free social services) and not directly connected with individual labor performance. In order to cope with this problem, in 1971 the government introduced the "Plan CTC-CI." Under this plan, consumer durables (such as television sets, refrigerators, washing machines, radios, bicycles, sewing machines, pressure cookers, watches) are not available in stores but allocated by the Ministry of Domestic Trade to enterprises. A list of available goods is put on a bulletin board of the enterprise and workers who are interested fill out forms. A committee of workers ranks the applicants mainly by their attitudes and merits (e.g., fulfillment of work quotas, productivity) and, to a lesser extent, by their need.[55]

The above policy is also applicable to vacations in beach resorts and, particularly, to the distribution of housing. The acute shortage of housing, especially in Havana and other cities, has been generated by the disappearance of all private construction in 1960 and the drastic curtailment of state housing construction *circa* 1962. To put a halt to the growing housing gap, at least 100,000 new homes are needed annually, but only a few were built in the 1960s. According to Castro, nine out of every ten people who approach him have housing problems; there are as many as ten people living in one room, couples who get divorces cannot move, and many couples cannot get married because they have no place to live. The distribution of houses, Castro has reported, has caused disorders, irregularities, and discontent. People have moved into houses without permission, and, in other cases, the distribution was unfair.[56] The exodus of Cubans to the United States helped to ease the problem, but in 1971 the Cuban government restricted the exit. It was suspended for six months in 1972, reestablished at lower levels by the end of that year, and stopped in mid-1973, thus closing the safety valve.

In mid-1971, Castro proposed a plan to reduce the housing shortage. The state would supply construction materials, and industrial workers would provide the manpower in two ways: regular workers would donate two or three daily hours of overtime plus Saturdays and Sundays; and surplus labor released in enterprises through "norming" could permanently work in housing construction while the rest of the workers would donate extra labor, if necessary, to maintain the production level. Apparently, the second system has been the most used, but the government has been careful to avoid depleting workers whose absence could harm production. By August 1971, 100 "minibrigades" enrolling 3,000 workers were organized. Minibrigades increased gradually to reach 1,068 in number enrolling 35,000 workers two years later. Each minibrigade is integrated by some 33 members who work from 10 to 15 hours daily. By mid-1973 the minibrigades had built 6,385 homes and had 37,500 more under construction (others built schools, day-care centers, and clinics). At the beginning of the program, ten minibrigades claimed a right to the houses built by them. Thereafter it was established that the homes would belong to the work centers so that "a close link will be established between the productive unit [enterprise] and the homes in which its workers live." Houses are distributed (for rent, not ownership, at 6 percent of wages) according to the merits (mainly productivity) of the workers and, to a lesser extent, according to their need. The government expects that under this program from 70,000 to 80,000 homes will be built annually beginning in 1975.[57]

In the spring of 1974, the predominance of moral incentives as a peculiarity of Cuban socialism had been clearly eliminated (at least for the Cubans). Some American social scientists who had strongly supported Castro's emphasis on moral incentives in 1966–1970, despite the negative economic consequences associated therewith, still refused to accept the current reality. For example, Harvard economics professor Arthur MacEwan, after an elaborate academic exercise, labeled the old terminology of "material" versus "moral" incentives as being "inaccurate" and substituted it with the dichotomy "personal" versus "collective." Omitting practically all the dramatic changes which have occurred in this area during 1970 to 1973, MacEwan, at the 1973 meetings of the American Economic

Association, sustained that: "while the actual system of incentives in Cuba is a composite of collective and personal factors, it appears that the collective incentives are dominant. Furthermore, one can see the emergence of the logic of collective incentives . . ."[58]

Rationalizing the Sugar Sector

The economic dislocation of 1970 was caused by the excessive emphasis placed on the sugar sector at the cost of sacrificing the rest of the economy. The nation's infrastructure and resources (sugar-mill equipment, harvest combines, transportation, skilled manpower) were obviously insufficient to reach the ten-million-ton target; even more, they were incapable of producing much more than six million tons without a harmful depletion of resources from other sectors. The too-ambitious goal wrecked part of the mills, and they were not repaired or replaced in 1971–1972.[59] Facing reality, sugar production targets have been gradually reduced, labor mobilization has sharply declined, and emphasis has been placed on finding adequate alternatives (such as the Australian system for burning the cane) and improving and expanding the mechanization.

The 1965–1970 sugar plan called for an investment of more than $1 billion in expansion and modernization of the sugar mills, but by 1970 only $400 million had materialized. Modernization was apparently postponed in 1971–1972 due to delays in the supply of machinery. In 1959, there were 161 sugar mills (mostly built before the end of the 1920s); but ten years later due to deterioration, lack of spare parts, and "cannibalization," the number of mills declined to 152. The strenuous effort to which the old equipment was subjected in the 1970 harvest put four other mills out of operation, and in the 1971 harvest frequent breakdowns were reported in the active mills. At the beginning of the 1972 harvest, it was announced that 144 mills would be in operation; but by the end of February only 136 were functioning and two months later only 115 mills were active.

The number of professional canecutters declined from 350,000 in 1958 to less than 73,000 in 1971. Mobilization of urban workers ("volunteers") could not adequately substitute for the professional canecutters due to the lack of the volunteers' expertise and their low productivity. In addition, the excessive depletion of urban manpower for use in the 1970 crop (some 170,000 men) precipitated an acute fall in industrial output. Some 60,000 fewer volunteers were mobilized in the 1971 harvest, another 35,000 less in the 1972 harvest, and 25,000 in the 1973 harvest. (The government expects to reduce total manpower in the 1980 harvest to 50,000 workers.) The number of days of the harvest declined from 334 in 1970 to 230 in 1972. (The participation of thousands of university students in the 1969–1970 sugar harvests for periods of from two to four months was quietly but drastically cut in the 1971–1972 harvests because their time was more usefully spent in studying.)[60]

Unpaid voluntary labor, in general, was limited in 1973 by the CTC Congress to tasks which are proven necessary; specifically, for the sugar harvest. Unions should select the most productive canecutters so as to reduce the number of volunteers. Often in the past the cost of mobilizing volunteers (transportation, food, electric power, inputs) was higher than the value of the product created by them.[61] Now such costs must be calculated in advance because if "what is accomplished does not compensate for the material and human resources invested, the mobilization would be uneconomical and wasteful." Unions that decide to use voluntary labor must carefully quantify the factors in the mobilization: number of workers, tools, transportation, food, shelter, inputs and work quotas. On the basis of all these factors, an analysis must be done of the efficiency of the work performed. The news media should abstain from publicizing volunteer-labor activities unless enough data are provided to measure their productivity.[62]

 Mechanization of the sugar harvest, the rational alternative to massive labor mobilization, has been "a very difficult nut to crack" as Castro has acknowledged. (On the other hand, the total mechanization of harvesting rice and potatoes is almost complete.) In 1967 a National Direction of Mechanization (DINAME) was created in the National Institute of Agrarian Reform (INRA); this agency was to be in charge of mechanization, importation of equipment, and repairs. The easiest task has been plowing; in 1970, there were 2,000 Cuban-made sugar plowers ("Herrera") in operation and half of the planting was mechanized. But some 1,000 Soviet-made cutting machines sent to Cuba in 1963–1965 were too heavy and complicated and broke easily; hence, they were discarded in 1967. (There was a futile attempt to put them back in operation for the 1970 harvest. The irregularity of the terrain presented a problem to the cutting machines. In 1972 work began to level large sugar plantations in Camagüey province—the flattest and the one with the higher manpower deficit.) Cuban-made cutting machines ("Henderson" and "Libertadora") were tested with fair results in 1967–1968, but they had to be mounted on imported bulldozers, and only a few could be built (e.g., 150 in 1969, while some 3,000 to 4,000 were needed). By the end of 1970, Castro complained that it was "one thing to make one machine by hand and quite another to turn them out in quantity and running perfectly."[63] In September 1971, Cuba bought 100 cutting machines from the Austrialian firm, Massey Ferguson, which were used in the 1972 crop (it was reported that a total of 250 machines were in operation in that harvest). Almost at the same time, at the first meeting of the Cuban-Soviet Commission, the U.S.S.R. agreed to help Cuba in manufacturing improved versions of the "Libertadora" and "Henderson" canecutting machines and to supply a new type of machine (called KTP-1) designed by Soviet and Cuban engineers based on the experience of the 1971 harvest. In mid-1972 the U.S.S.R. announced that a new factory to build KPT-1 machines would be sent to Cuba; fifty of these machines built in the Soviet Union were tested in the 1973 sugar harvest. Early in 1973 it was reported that the construction of the KTP-1 factory in Cuba would begin in Holguín (Oriente province) during that year. First it was said that the factory would produce 600 machines annually, but, later the figure was reduced to 300–400 machines and finally to 200–300 machines. The government estimated that 420 machines (Libertadora, Henderson, Massey-Ferguson, KTP-1) operated in the 1973 harvest, increasing the mechanization process from 7 percent in 1972 to 11–12 percent in 1973.[64] It is expected that by 1980 the harvest will be 80-percent mechanized.

The small number of cutting machines currently in operation is compounded by their incapacity to clean the cane of leaves and trash (only the "Libertadora" allegedly does this work), which amounts to half the volume of the cane cut. Cane-cleaning centers (which mechanically strip the cane of leaves) were tested in 1966; by the end of 1971 some 200 had been built and 300 other centers were scheduled to be built for the 1972 harvest. If these had been built, they could have cleaned half of the whole cut cane, but it was reported that only 20 percent of the cane was actually processed through the centers. Loading of the cut cane (into carts, railroad wagons) was mechanized by 80–90 percent in 1973, with some 4,000 lifters mounted on old American tractors and imported Soviet cranes made for this purpose. In late 1971, the U.S.S.R. agreed to send Cuba 1,600 carts (2-PTT-6) to be used for transporting sugar in the 1972 harvest, and a factory to produce these carts began to be built in early 1973 increasing motorized transportation to 60 percent.

Trying to ease some of the above problems, in the 1970 harvest the Center for Research on Sugar Cane conducted an investigation of the Australian system of burning and cutting cane.[65] (Besides Australia, the system has also been used in the last twenty or thirty years in Hawaii, Mexico, Peru, and South Africa.) The Australian system was tested on a minor scale in January-February 1971; thereafter, 60 percent of the cane was burned.[66] The system apparently saved considerable manpower, as much as 62 percent. The burned cane did not have to be cleaned of leaves and dirt, it was not recut into two pieces, it weighed less, and did not have to be piled.

Conversely, the Australian system created new complications. In order to have the system work properly, the terrain had to be prepared, a special variety of cane was needed (to have stalks of equal size), replanting had to be done more frequently, the seed had to be planted at a given depth and separation, and special fertilizer had to be used. The burning process had to be carefully planned: a schedule had to be prepared based on the degree of maturity of the cane, the burning had to take place at sunset, and excessive burning which provokes losses in sugar and incomplete burning which leaves the trash in the plant had to be avoided. There was also always the risk of fire expansion and losses resulting from leaving the burned cane in the fields too long before being ground. Since the cane was neither recut into two pieces (as done manually) nor piled up, there were problems with the traditional equipment in use. Cranes faced difficulties in picking up the unpiled cane. The long cane stalks stuck in the too-narrow railroad cars which transported 70 percent of the cane to the mills. In the cane-cutting centers, the engines overheated and, in some cases, burned. The machete, the most popular Cuban tool for cutting cane, which is used in 58 percent of the harvest, was too long and narrow; and the Australian tool (shorter and wider) was disliked by the cane-cutters. Finally, special clothing and safety devices (steel padding to protect the legs and reinforced gloves) had to be introduced; the workers rejected the gloves because they reduced their movements and hurt their hands.

In late 1971, several measures were tested to cope with some of these difficulties. For instance, a "pusher" was attached to the crane machines to pile up the cane; the cane was cut into two pieces in the cleaning centers; to avoid engines overheating in the centers, the speed of the feeder belts was reduced; Chinese cutters (smaller and wider than the machete, similar to the "mochas" traditionally used in 32 percent of the Cuban harvest) were tried; and gloves were eliminated. This resulted in a modified Australian system which is claimed to be twice as productive as the traditional methods used in Cuba although only one-third as productive as the pure Australian system.

No information is available on the results of the application of the modified Australian system in the 1972 sugar harvest, but there are data on the industrial yield which suggest that things did not go as well as expected. (The industrial yield is the percentage of sugar obtained in the mills in relation to the weight of the cut cane. Out of every 100 tons of cane cut, from 8 to 14 tons of raw sugar are squeezed, depending on the cleansing of the leaves from the cane, the sugar content of the cane, and the efficiency of the mill equipment.) The prerevolutionary yield was systematically above 12 percent, but it went down to 11.8 percent in 1965–1969. The yield in the 1970 harvest was a very low one, 10.9 percent, mainly attributed to the excessively large crop. In the 1971 harvest, the yield rose to 11.5 percent, but it went down to 10.5 percent in the 1972 harvest.[67] Drought could not be held responsible for the difference because it affected both crops; in fact, there was less rain during the period of cane maturation of the 1971 crop than in that of the 1972 crop. The deteriorating equipment could have been a cause, but not an important one if we assume that those mills that had functioning difficulties were not in operation in 1972. (This probably affected the total amount of the crop but not necessarily its yield.) There was a significant difference in the two crops: the Australian system applied in less than one-third of the 1971 harvest but throughout the 1972 harvest. Probably improper burning, bottlenecks caused by the insufficient number of cane-conditioning centers, and difficulties generated by the use of the new technique resulted in loss in the sugar content of the cane. Nothing has been published on the Australian system in the 1973 sugar harvest.

On July 1, 1972, President Dorticós announced that beginning in 1973 Cuba would not attempt to produce large sugar crops but only the amount of sugar that the country could rationally turn out.[68] The Ministry of Sugar reported at the same time that repairs and maintenance of the sugar mills would receive priority in 1973. Later it was stated that fertilizers will be increased by 30 percent in 1974.[69] And the president of the National Academy of Sciences announced that in 1973–1977 electronic calculation would be used in sugar production.[70] The trend toward rationality seems to continue, but the role that the Australian system will play in the future is not clear.

Impact of the New Policies on Production

Two years is a very short span in which to evaluate the results of the Cuban shift toward economic pragmatism, particularly if it is realized that some of the changes are still in experimental stages. The lack of systematic and accurate data (or, even worse, the complete absence of some data since 1966) makes the task even more difficult.[71] Therefore, the following information, from Castro's speeches, the official news media, and non-Cuban sources should be taken very cautiously.

Data on GNP (actually gross *material* product, which excludes the value of part of the services sector) published by JUCEPLAN cover only the period of 1962–1967 and show steady increases in

1963–1965 but declines in 1966–1967 when Sino-Guevarism was fully implemented. GNP at constant prices in 1967 was 2 percent below GNP in 1962 (a year of recession) and 14 percent below GNP in 1965 (a fairly good economic year). In per capita terms, the deterioration was worse, with the 1967 GNP level 13 percent below that of 1962 and 17 percent below that of 1965.[72] The World Bank recently released estimates on Cuba's GNP per capita which suggest a further deterioration in 1969.[73] British publications have reported that GNP in 1970 was about the same as 1969 and 7 percent below that of 1968.[74] The picture that emerges from these estimates (as well as from data on agricultural and industrial output to be discussed below) is that GNP declined steadily in 1966–1969 and became stagnant in 1970. It would not be too adventurous to set the total GNP decline in 1966–1970 at some 30 percent, a high cost indeed for the Sino-Guevarist experiment. There are no accurate figures on GNP for 1971–1973, and data on agricultural and industrial output are too incomplete and contradictory to allow any serious GNP estimate. Nevertheless, top Cuban officials have reported an increase of GNP by 2.5–5.0 percent in 1971, by 9–10 percent in 1972, and by 13–17 percent in 1973.[75] (See table 3.)

Throughout the first decade of the Revolution, there was fairly good performance in industry. In a comparison of output in 1957–1958 and 1967–1968, there were increases in fish (200 percent); crude oil, nickel ore, evaporated and condensed milk, cigarettes, paper and board (100 percent); and electricity and salt (40 percent). Production of gas, cement, beer, footwear, and cigars was stagnant, and there were declines in the output of copper, manganese, chrome, tires and tubes, and rayon and acetate filaments. But if one concentrates on the period 1965–1968, a continuing trend of increasing output is observed until 1968 (the Year of the Revolutionary Offensive) when a dramatic decline occurred. While in 1967 there were output increases in 80 percent of the most important industrial products (minerals, energy, manufacturing, food), in 1968 there were decreases in 50 percent of those products, stagnation in another 20 percent, and increases in only 30 percent of them.[76] Official statistics analyzed below, although scarce and incomplete, suggest that industrial output deteriorated further in 1969–1970, but

TABLE 3

Estimates of Economic Growth in Cuba: 1971-1973
(In percentage of variation in each year from previous year)

Years	GNP[a] Castro	GNP[a] Dorticós-Rodríguez	Industry (excludes sugar)	Sugar[d]
1971	5	2.5	---	-30.6
1972	9	10	14	-24.5[e]
1973	13[b]	17[b]	15[c]	20.0

[a]Probably Gross Material Product (GMP)

[b]Estimate

[c]January-September

[d]Physical output

[e]Based on the highest estimate of production available

Sources: *GNP* from O. Dorticós, "Control económico y perspectivas del desarrollo de la economía cubana," *Economía y Desarrollo,* no. 11 (May-June 1972), p. 11, and "Desarrollar cultural, científica y técnicamente los cuadros administrativos," ibid., no. 20 (November-December 1973), p. 54; C. R. Rodríguez, "Speech at the 15th Session of ECLA in Quito, Ecuador," *Granma Weekly Review,* April 8, 1973, p. 9; and F. Castro, "Discurso en el acto de clausura del XIII Congreso de la CTC," *Juventud Rebelde,* November 16, 1973, p. 6. *Industry* from C. R. Rodríguez, "Interview in Hungary," *Granma Weekly Review,* December 16, 1973, p. 10. *Sugar* from discussion and sources in the text.

almost recuperated the 1967 level in 1971 and surpassed that level in 1972. (See table 4.)

Information for 1971 is available in detail for only three industrial ministries. Basic industry reported output increases over 1970 in refrigeration (200 percent), machinery construction (46 percent), and steel (18 percent), breaking output records in the first and third. There was fulfillment or overfulfillment of output targets in two-thirds of the products including air conditioning, ventilators, metal shaping, telephone wire, and glass containers. The Ministry of Mining, Fuels, and Metallurgy reported a record output and increase over 1970 in salt (41 percent) and fulfillment or overfulfillment of output targets in two-thirds of its products including nickel and copper but excluding oil. The Ministry of Light Industry reported an

TABLE 4

Percentage Increase in Industrial Output in the First Quarter of 1972 Over
the First Quarter of 1971 and in the Year 1971 Over the Year 1970

Sector	1972/1971	1971/1970
Steel	74	18
Construction	68	25
Tobacco	60	——*
Machinery	50	46
Construction materials	43	41
Metallurgy and mechanics	38	42
Refrigeration	——	200
Salt	——	41
Beverages	37	23
Fishing	23	18
Electric power	14	7
Textiles and leather	14	18
Oil refining	10	3
Chemicals	7	15
Food	4	10
Mining	6	0

*Tobacco declined substantially, possibly by 40 percent.

Sources: For 1972, F. Castro, "Speech at the May Day Parade and Workers' Rally held in the Plaza de la Revolución, May 1, 1972," *Granma Weekly Review,* May 7, 1972, p. 2; and "Cuba económica," *Economía y Desarrollo,* no. 16 (March-April 1973), pp. 203-11. For 1971: *Granma Weekly Review,* January 30, 1972, pp. 8-10; "Cuba económica," *Economía y Desarrollo,* no. 10 (March-April 1972), pp. 177-81; and O. Dorticós, "Control económico y normación: tareas de primer orden," *Economía y Desarrollo,* no. 11 (May-June 1972), pp. 17-18.

overall increase in output of 20 percent over 1970 (setting eight output records) and fulfillment or overfulfillment of output targets in half of its products (including furniture but excluding footwear, textiles, plastics, and cosmetics). Success was officially attributed to repairs and better maintenance; improved organization in the supply of inputs, transportation, and coordination; and introduction of work quotas, decreases in mobilization and absenteeism, and increase in labor productivity.[77]

In the first quarter of 1972, increases in output over the same period of 1971 were reported in practically all industrial products: steel (74 percent), construction (68 percent), machinery (50 percent), construction materials (43 percent), metallurgy and mechanics (38 percent), electric power, textiles, and leather (14 percent), oil refining (10 percent), chemicals (7 percent), tobacco (60 percent), beverages (37 percent), fishing (23 percent), and food (4 percent).[78] The output of electricity probably increased even more in the second half of 1972 due to the addition of an electrical unit to the old Havana plant which increased the capacity by 60,000 kilowatt hours.[79] Figures released on industrial output for the whole year of 1972 are incomplete and difficult to compare with those published for the first quarter of the year. Nevertheless, they suggest a remarkable increase in 1972 over 1971 although in some cases at lower rates than reported for the first quarter (e.g., 48 percent in steel, 25 percent in beverages, 11 percent in fishing) and in other cases at higher rates (e.g., 10 percent in food, 44 percent in construction materials).[80] Rodríguez has reported that non-sugar industrial output increased by 14 percent in 1972 and by 15 percent in the first nine months of 1973.[81]

Agriculture, and especially sugar, the backbone of the Cuban economy, has had a discouragingly bad performance under the Revolution, especially since 1961. Output in 1967–1968 was either below or remained the same as that of 1957–1958 except for a few products which showed increases: eggs (300 percent), tomatoes (200 percent), onions (100 percent), citrus fruits (50 percent), and potatoes and poultry (10–20 percent).[82] According to FAO, total agricultural output in 1969 was 7 percent below that of 1958; and if per capita figures are used, the decline was 25 percent.[83] In 1970 sugar output set a record of 8.5 million tons, but this was partly offset by declines in all other agricultural products except eggs and rice. The Cuban delegation to the 1971 meeting of FAO (Food and Agriculture Organization) acknowledged declines in output in 1970 over 1966 of 21 percent in non-sugar agriculture and 6 percent in livestock, but an overall agricultural output increase of 30 percent.[84] (This was the result of the 90 percent increase in sugar output in 1970 over the very bad year of 1966; but if the annual output rates for the five years had been averaged, the figures would have been dramatically different.) Agricultural production in 1971 was affected by a severe drought, and there were declines in the output of sugar, livestock, and tobacco. The situation in 1972 was difficult to evaluate due to the lack of data; there were reports of a very bad sugar crop but of scattered increases in output in non-sugar agriculture.

The original sugar target for the 1971 crop was set by Castro at the end of 1970: "The rock-bottom minimum is seven million tons, and even this still means great imbalances." But on May Day 1971, he reduced the target to 6.5 million tons, warning that "less than that amount would adversely affect our foreign exchange receipts."[85] Final output was 5.9 million tons, some 3 million tons less than in 1970 and 10 percent below the second target. The government set a goal of 5.2 million tons for the 1972 sugar crop but did not report output results (it said only that the harvest was below the 5 million tons).[86] Estimates from Eastern European diplomats and British and West German sources ranged from 3.5 to 4.5 million tons.[87] This was, probably, the second lowest harvest of the Revolution—the 1963 crop produced 3.9 million tons. According to the Minister of Foreign Trade, Marcelo Fernández, the 1973 sugar crop was a fair one: 5.4 million tons.[88] The 1974 harvest promises to be a fair one and will be favored by increasing sugar prices in the international market.[89] The negative performance in the sugar sector has partly offset the advances in other sectors, particularly in 1971. In this year, non-sugar production increased by 17 percent, but sugar production declined by 31 percent, and the rate of GNP growth was probably 2.5 percent.[90]

In 1967 there were almost 7 million head of cattle but thereafter the number declined reaching a low of 5 million in 1970 which remained stagnant in 1971 due to a low birth rate and an increase in the mortality rate.[91] Various technical reports published in 1969–1971 by British genetic advisors of the Cuban government suggest a bad performance in this sector due to failures in the breeding and artificial insemination programs, poor quality of fodder, cattle illnesses, and drought.[92] Output of pork declined sharply in 1971–1972 due to a grave epidemic of African Fever (or "Pig Cholera"), which in mid–1971 rapidly spread throughout Havana province. As a result, 410,000 hogs had to be killed, leaving only 36,000 in the province.[93] Production of poultry in 1972 was probably stagnant. On the other hand, the government reported that the procurement quota *("acopio")* of raw milk increased by 9 percent in 1971 and by 50 percent in 1972; this permitted increases in yogurt and ice cream and the resumption of butter production.[94]

Tobacco output was seriously affected by a drought in 1970–1971. In 1971, the rainfall in the tobacco growing areas of Vuelta Abajo, Pinar del Rio province, was one-fifth the average rainfall, and 40 percent of the crop was lost. But in 1972 the situation seemed to improve considerably with a reported increase of 60 percent of output in the first quarter of that year. The government expects to regain the 1961 record of tobacco output by 1975. Production of eggs increased by 5 percent in 1971 but only by 2.3 percent in 1972. Production of rice and citrus fruits in 1972 was about 10 percent below the target and the tomato crop was a bad one.[95] Little is known of other agricultural products. There is an official report stating that private agricultural output (in the small private farms that produce most tobacco, tubers, vegetables, fruits, and coffee) had increased by 71 percent in the first quarter of 1972.[96] It was expected that Castro would release some data on sugar output and other agricultural products in his speech of July 26, 1972. But the speech was devoted mainly to foreign policy and only in one paragraph, the last, were internal conditions mentioned, when he said that "everything is going fine."[97] In Castro's subsequent speeches until the end of 1973 he did not release any new statistics on agricultural output.

Evaluation and Prospectives

Bearing in mind the cautions expressed above (too short a period of observation and lack of data), it may be said that the new economic policy toward pragmatism, inaugurated in 1970, has been followed by good performance in industry and fishing but with bad performance in sugar and not-too-impressive performance in non-sugar agriculture. A factor that may largely explain the different outcome is the drought, one of the worst in the century, which reduced water in dams from one-fourth to one-half their average level.[98] Illnesses that affected livestock could have been significant also. Another reason is that in order to restore output in an economy seriously dislocated by the 1970 sugar-harvest mobilization, it was necessary to drastically cut the depletion of manpower from industry and this had to affect the sugar sector. The application in large scale of the Australian system in the 1972 sugar harvest and the deteriorating equipment may have affected output also. Still a third reason is that industrial output and productivity, especially in modern, concentrated factories, can be easily and rapidly increased with Soviet aid, repairs and maintenance, improved organization and control of labor output (e.g., work quotas), but this is not so easy in the dispersed, backward, unpredictable agricultural sector. Most of the economic incentives introduced in 1971–1973 (e.g., more consumer goods available, the housing program) appeal fundamentally to the urban worker but not to rural workers and private farmers. Last but not least is that fact that the shift toward pragmatism has not been decisive enough and may have been negatively affected by the 1971–1973 tightening of political control.

Assuming that the current pragmatist trend continues unchanged, prospectives in terms of overall economic growth should be positive although not spectacular. The prime minister has said in this respect: "The objectives of our people in the material field cannot be very ambitious. . . . We should work in the next ten years to advance our economy at an average annual growth rate of six percent."[99] The performance of Cuban production in the next three or four years can be prudently predicted as follows: in the sugar sector, fair-sized crops of from five to six million tons probably aided by high prices in the international market (mechanization should expand in the late 1970s and crops may reach seven million tons); in non-sugar agriculture, recuperation of previous output (e.g., in tobacco) and possibly more advances in mechanized harvests (e.g., rice, potatoes, tomatoes) or modern enterprises (e.g., poultry, eggs); in livestock, stagnant output of meat but increases in milk; in fishing, continuous steady increases in output; and in industry, steady and moderate increases especially in the dynamic sector (basic industry, mining—particularly nickel—

fuel, metallurgy, and electricity). Production of steel will not be initiated until the 1980s.

To obtain more impressive results, the government would have to take more decisive steps. For instance, the percentage of GMP devoted to consumption could be increased with only 25 percent saved for investment purposes; this reduction may be compensated for by increasing capital efficiency (through better planning) and labor productivity (by a combination of work quotas and better incentives). A general reform of the price system is necessary for a more rational allocation of capital, intermediate, and consumer goods. Price reform and a better supply of consumer goods would eliminate rationing and the remnants of socialist inflation. The reintroduction of self-financing in most of the economy but especially in agriculture would help improve efficiency and productivity. This objective could be reinforced by using profit as the main indicator of managerial performance and of the interest rate (or a similar device) as the main mechanism for allocating capital. In agriculture, the procurement quota *("acopio")* imposed on private farmers could be reduced and the fixed state price for their products increased, and an *ad hoc* system of incentives for rural wage earners would have to be implemented.

3

Government and Society: Towards Institutionalization

At the end of the 1960s, the political structure of Cuba became the target of criticism from several Marxist and leftist sympathizers of the Revolution. They claimed that decision making was done by Fidel Castro and a small group of followers and that he was reluctant to delegate his power. The party and the unions had almost withered away, the government elite imposed its will upon the masses without consultation, and Cuban society had gradually become militarized. Therefore it was urgent to reform the system and develop socialist democratic institutions. Be it the result of this criticism or the effect of other causes, in the second half of 1970 Fidel Castro acknowledged some of the flaws pinpointed by his critics and promised dramatic reforms to decentralize the state administration, revitalize and democratize the labor movement and other mass organizations, and allow mass participation in decision making and the supervision of state functions.

This chapter begins with a summary of both the Marxist criticism and Castro's promises of reform. This is followed by a thorough description of the reforms undertaken in 1971–1973 aimed at the separation of governmental functions, the reorganization and democratization of the unions and other mass organizations, and the introduction of participatory types of institutions. In addition, there is a discussion of measures, taken simultaneously, that have strengthened government control over the workers, small farmers, the youth, and the intellectuals. The chapter ends with an analysis of the type of institutionalization that is taking place in Cuba, confronting two opposite trends: one towards decentralization and democratization and another towards centralization and rigidity in ideology, culture, and education.

The Marxist Criticism of the Political Structure

In the midst of Cuba's "Revolutionary Offensive" (1968–1969), several Marxist scholars visited the island, the majority of them invited by Prime Minister Fidel Castro.[1] The visitors, internationally known in various specialties and from Europe and the United States, had all previously been in Cuba—some as consultants of the government—and had thereafter published sympathetic accounts of the revolutionary accomplishments. They had something else in common: their endorsement of a more democratic, participatory type of socialism. If they originally expected to find in Cuba the kind of socialism that they dreamed of, their books and articles published in 1969 and 1970, although supportive of the Cuban Revolution in general, showed their disappointment in this respect.

The American economists Paul Sweezy and the late Leo Huberman were the first to state that the Cuban Revolution was moving close to autocracy and to recommend, as an alternative, the participation of the people in decisions and responsibilities.[2] In a controversy with Sweezy, the French planner and ideologist, Charles Bettelheim, criticized the Cuban leaders as a section of the petty bourgeoisie that had concentrated all powers unto itself, thus becoming a class. He further charged that it had imposed its political domination upon the masses, curtailing their independent movements; and that it had done nothing to create the necessary conditions—ideological, political and organizational—for the democratic exercise of proletarian power.[3]

The American sociologist, Maurice Zeitlin, found that the Cuban Communist Party (PCC) did not have real power and that trade unions seemed to have withered away. He also stated: "The Cuban revolutionaries have so far done little to establish institutions to guarantee that competing points of view can be heard within the revolutionary socialist consensus; that meaningful alternatives are debated; that policies are initiated, as well as implemented by the citizenry at large." Zeitlin concluded that the Cubans had to choose between autocracy and the establishment of socialist democratic political forms.[4]

In his third visit to Cuba, René Dumont, the French agronomist, observed that the lack of confidence in the base, Castro's reluctance to delegate responsibility, and the making of all important decisions at the top of the administrative hierarchy had resulted in increasing personalism, paternalism, and authoritarianism. Central controls had been imposed on the population, the universities, and the press; and there was expanding militarization of education, manpower, agriculture, the economy, and society in general. Dumont suggested that Castro give up some of his powers or otherwise be induced to do so by his responsible colleagues; that the administration be simplified and that more autonomy and initiative be given to local units; and that fundamental issues be publicly discussed and the party and state agencies controlled by the worker.[5]

The Polish-British journalist and writer, K. S. Karol, asserted that by 1968 all mass organizations in Cuba had ceased to exist except on paper, that the unions were neither autonomous nor had the right to express and defend the claims of their members, and that the Cuban rulers believed that they knew best how to interpret the thoughts and needs of the working class. According to Karol, Castro disagreed with both China's Cultural Revolution and the Czech Spring of 1968 because he was afraid of changes initiated by uncontrolled and spontaneous forces and suspicious of rank-and-file independent action.[6]

In mid-1970, in the midst of the economic dislocation, widespread labor absenteeism, and popular disenchantment that followed the sugar crop failure, the Cuban leadership seemed to reconsider its previous attitudes. On July 26, Castro acknowledged his own errors; in August he announced the "new phase" of the Revolution; and in the fall he proposed several measures that, deliberately or not, were addressed to the correction of most of the defects indicated by his Marxist critics.

The 1970 Promises of Reform

From May through December 1970, Castro made numerous speeches in which he strongly criticized the excessive centralization of the administration and its bureaucratization, the absorption of administrative functions by the PCC, the exaggerated role of the state in all national affairs (which killed the initiative of the masses), the one-manager system of state enterprises (which did not allow the workers to express their opinions), and the weak and non-democratic state of mass organizations. He proposed several measures to decentralize the administration, assign separate roles to key state agencies, allow the workers to participate in enterprise management, democratize and strengthen mass organizations, and establish channels for a more active role of such organizations in national affairs.

First Castro proclaimed that in the future the PCC's role would be restricted to the coordination and supervision of the administrative function.[7] To separate political and administrative functions within the PCC, Castro proposed that in the Central Committee, besides the political bureau, there be a "bureau of social production" to coordinate the activities of the administration. In another move, Castro acknowledged that it was no longer possible to direct all national production through the Council of Ministers alone and announced the clustering of various central ministries with connected functions into groups that would help in the planning and coordination of such functions. Thus a group would deal with capital (or intermediate) goods production (the Ministry of Basic Industry; and the Ministry of Mining, Fuel, and Metallurgy); another group with consumer-goods production and distribution (Ministries of Food Industry, Light Industry, and Domestic Trade); and another with manpower (Ministries of Labor, Education, and Armed Forces). At a third level, Castro said that the administration of the enterprise would not be the task of the manager alone but of a "collective body" presided over by the manager and integrated by representatives of the workers, the party, and youth and female organizations.[8] A few days later Minister of Labor Jorge Risquet stated: "The administrator may be making one mistake after the other, and this happens every day, everywhere. . . . The workers cannot do anything about it. . . . How can the worker be made to feel more involved with his place of employment, with his production goal if he is only a producer who never has any opinion, who cannot make any decision, who is never consulted about factory management?" Risquet also said that forms of participation were under discussion so that output plans and long-term decisions in the enterprise could be discussed with the workers.[9]

Mass participation would not be limited to the enterprise alone, Castro proclaimed: "We must begin to substitute democratic methods for the administrative methods that run the risk of becoming bureaucratic."[10] The democratization process would be the basis for the participation of the masses in decision making, and all mass organizations would go through such a process.[11] He acknowledged that the trade union movement was in poor shape and should be revitalized through democratization (free elections); it should also be allowed to defend the workers' rights. Other mass organizations (e.g., youth, farmers, women) would follow the democratization of the unions. Castro went further: "Starting with our mass organizations [we will] create other organizations in which the workers, the women, the young people will be represented so that they carry out close supervision and control of all activities [including those of the party] on a territorial level."[12]

At the end of the year, Castro elaborated on his participatory scheme: "[Why has everything] to be administered directly by the state?. . . . Immediately the need arises for the superorganization [which makes the citizen indifferent]. . . . We believe that this is wrong. . . . And it is up to us to create the links and the mechanisms through which the citizen will be made to feel his duty and to take an interest in these matters." The central agencies should handle only those functions that, because of their national character, had to be centralized, while other functions should be transferred to city-district bodies integrated by representatives of the workers and of youth, women's and student organizations. Castro gave an example of how this could be accomplished: "[The Ministry of Domestic Trade] should continue running the wholesale distribution and laying down the guidelines for the distribution of goods, but it should be relieved of the job of running a grocery store. . . . It is the representatives of the mass organizations who should handle the things that pertain to the community." He reported an experiment developed in the small town of Peñalver, east of Havana, in which some eight neighbors working every day until 11:00 p.m., with construction equipment and material supplied by the state, built a baseball field and a communal garage and repaired some roads. But he warned that before mobilizing the energy of the masses the necessary time had to be taken to carefully study the proposed undertaking.[13]

Separation of Government Functions: The Administration, the Party, and the Army

When in 1970 Castro acknowledged the need to separate the functions of the administration and the party, he was only referring to part of the problem. The main feature of the Cuban political structure in the 1960s was extreme diffusion; there was no clear separation among the following three main institutions and their functions: the central administration, the party, and the army. Castro exerted a charismatic, personalistic type of government characterized by the concentration of power in the "Maximum Leader" and his inner circle of loyalists and by the lack of institutionalization. The Council of Ministers, headed by Castro and integrated by his closest associates, controlled the administration which performed executive, legislative, and judicial functions. Most ministers and directors of central agencies, nevertheless, came from the Rebel Army. The party, except in its brief period of inception (1961 to early 1962 when PSP members had strong influence), was in Castroite hands. In 1965, two-thirds of the PCC Central Committee members were from military ranks. In practice, Castro and his small circle occupied the top positions in the administration, the party, and the army; he was the best example combining the jobs of prime minister, first secretary of the party, and commander-in-chief of the armed forces. The latter was probably the only body that, in spite of constant changes and crises, grew increasingly professionalized, institutionalized, and efficient. Thus the army absorbed more and more non-military functions (e.g., organization of production, criticism of rebel intellectuals, cane cutting) and by the end of the decade pervaded many facets of Cuban society.[14] The changes being introduced in the 1970s indicate that the announced separation of functions within the government is not only limited to the administration and the party but to the army as well. In addition, each of the three institutions is going through a reorganization process whose main traits are: delegation of power but central coordination in the administration, revitalization in the party and specialization in the army. The general trend in the 1970s appears to be toward institutionalization following the Soviet model.

The creation of the Executive Committee of the Council of Ministers at the end of 1972 seems to be a step forward in the delegation of power from the prime minister and central coordination (see chapter 1). The Committee is integrated by the prime minister as chairman and nine "deputy prime ministers," a post typical of the Soviet hierarchy that did not previously exist in Cuba. Each of the deputies coordinates several ministries and state agencies which are clustered by sectors, i.e., basic industry and energy; consumer-goods industries and domestic trade; sugar industry; non-sugar agriculture; construction; transportation and communication; labor, planning, and foreign trade; foreign relations; and education and culture.[15] This measure had been announced by Castro in 1970 to better coordinate planning and production, and from an economic viewpoint (particularly if it is that of the central planners) it may prove to be effective.

The reorganization of executive powers was followed, in mid-1973, by the reform of both the judicial system and the criminal and procedural codes. The study of the reform, initiated in 1970 as part of the "new phase of the Revolution," was led by Blas Roca, a layman but former president of the PSP and, since 1965, chief of the Commission on Juridical Studies of the PCC.[16] The Commission is still working on a new political constitution and the reform of the Civil Code. The 1973 reform rejected the division of state powers into three branches—executive, legislative and judiciary—as a bourgeois institution and confirmed the Council of Ministers as "the supreme, the sole organ of power" embracing the three branches plus constitutional functions. The reform has placed the judicial system hierarchically subordinated to the executive. At the top of the former, there is a "Council of Government of the People's Supreme Court," which, instead of following the system of judicial independence for interpretation of the law, "transmits [to the lower judicial echelons] the instructions received from the leadership of the Revolution whose fulfillment is compulsory." The new judicial system unified the four branches of justice: ordinary, military, revolutionary (political crimes), and people's courts (minor offenses of a social nature).[17] Exempted from the jurisdiction of the unified courts are the president of the republic, the prime minister and other ministers, and the members of the PCC Political Bureau who can be tried only by special party courts.[18] Private law practice is to be abolished, and all lawyers are to abide by and promote the revolutionary ideology in their political and juridical relations. It is also expected that lawyers would "improve themselves ideologically" and be militantly behind revolutionary causes. Defendants in trials will only have a state lawyer, even in those cases in which the state is a party.[19]

The PCC has two executive branches at the national level: the Political Bureau and the General Secretariat, respectively integrated by eight and six members and both headed by Castro. The party's deliberative body is the Central Committee, integrated by some one hundred members. It should, theoretically, elect the members of the political bureau and the secretariat but these were appointed in 1965 and, apparently, new appointments (to fill vacancies caused by deaths and purges) have not been made thereafter. At the time of its inception the composition of the Central Committee was as follows: 67 percent military (including 57 majors), 26 percent professionals, and 7 percent workers. The executive and deliberative bodies of the PCC seldom met in the 1960s. There are also party secretariats in each of the six Cuban provinces, which in turn supervise smaller secretariats in districts and municipalities. Party cells are organized in most important enterprises, state farms, government offices, and military units. The party has never had a congress, lacks both a program and statutes, and has a tiny membership.[20]

In early 1973 an agreement was reached at the Council of

Ministers to determine the functions of the party and its relations with the administration; unfortunately the basic document has not been published. At the same time the General Secretariat was increased to ten members and the four new posts were filled (one of the new secretaries is the Cuban Ambassador to the U.S.S.R.).[21] Meetings of the PCC executive bodies have become regular: the secretariat meets weekly and the Political Bureau bimonthly. There is no information on Central Committee meetings. In early 1973, besides the 6 secretariats in the provinces, 60 were reported in districts, and 401 in municipalities, plus 14,360 in local cells.[22]

In 1969 there were only 55,000 party members; in the subsequent four years, quiet efforts began to increase party membership through selection of candidates, political education, and recruitment. The number of members jumped to 101,000 in 1971, increased to 122,000 in 1972, and reached 153,000 in March of 1973. In addition there were 30,000 candidates being trained in Havana province alone.[23] The PCC membership was still small in 1973 (equivalent to 1.7 percent of the population and 5.5 percent of the labor force) but had increased three-fold in less than four years. Reportedly there is also an effort to expand the proletariat segment of the membership.[24] Both party members and candidates are taking political education courses which closely follow the Soviet interpretation of Marxism.[25]

The first congress of the party was announced by Castro in 1966 for the following year but it did not take place. The congress was then rescheduled for 1969 but later cancelled on the allegation that all the nation's efforts had to be concentrated on the 1970 sugar harvest. In late 1973, Castro promised that the congress finally would take place in 1975 and, at the beginning of 1974, his brother Raúl reported that preparations for the congress were already being made.[26] Prior to the congress, drafts should be elaborated on the program and statutes of the party as well as on resolutions to be adopted by the congress. These are to be sent for discussion to provincial, district, and municipal secretariats and to local cells which should also elect delegates to the congress. The congress is expected to discuss and approve the national program of the party, the proper strategy to implement it, the party's internal statutes and the international political line, and national issues such as the

1976–1980 economic plan. The party's statutes should include the conditions for membership (one of which is complete acceptance of the party's program), the procedure to select members, the principles of "unity of action, strict discipline and inadmissibility of factions," and sanctions for those who commit grave mistakes or betray the party line. Finally, the congress should select the new Central Committee which will, in turn, choose the political bureau, and the secretariat.[27] There will then be a significant test of the seriousness of the current process of separation of administration and party functions and delegation of power from Castro: whether he would retain the positions of prime minister and first secretary of the party or yield the latter to somebody else.

Although not officially acknowledged, the armed forces have also undergone an important reorganization in the early 1970s.[28] Its ranks have been reduced but in concentrating on purely military activities have become increasingly specialized and hierarchical. Former army labor squads such as the remnants of the "Military Units to Aid Production" (UMAP) and the "Divisions of Permanent Infantry" (DIP) have been merged with civilian (although militarily organized) labor brigades as the "Youth Centennial Column" and the "Followers of Camilo and Che," into the new "Youth Army of Work" (EJT). This has been structured as a paramilitary agency of the Ministry of the Armed Forces (FAR) but completely separate from the regular army. One reason for this reorganization was the need for centralization to avoid "the proliferation of minicolumns that disperse and divert efforts, developing a structure parallel to that of the administrative leadership." Another was to institutionalize a selective process to strengthen the increasing professionalization of the army. The regular army will not be involved in production while the EJT will draft youngsters, who are neither fit for the army nor for study, into a three-year program of disciplinary training and work in agriculture.[29]

Another step in the direction of centralization of military activities has been the absorption and programmed phasing out of the militia. This paramilitary organization integrated by armed workers and peasants played a crucial role in consolidating the Revolution in its early years. Its fate was marked in 1963 when the compulsory military service was established; the following year the militia's arms were taken away by the army. Ten years later, in April 1973, all militiamen were put on military "reserve," given the honorary rank of sublieutenants of the FAR, received ID cards, and were ordered to change their grey uniforms for the traditional olive-green fatigues of the army. They may use the army uniforms only when performing official activities and while on active reserve. Once the latter expires, the militiamen's services will no longer be required.[30]

In the 1970s the trend for modernization and professionalization of the army has reached its highest point so far. The Soviet Union has supplied Cuba with the most modern weapons and trained Cuban military personnel in their use (see chapter 1). The ministers of defense or army chiefs of the U.S.S.R., Czechoslovakia, and Poland have visited Cuba and participated in military exercises. Raúl Castro has reciprocated these visits by traveling through Eastern Europe.

As a final outcome of this process, in late 1973 the officer corps of the Cuban armed forces had their ranking system reorganized into a more conventional hierarchy according to their growing complexity and status. To avoid and repudiate the escalation of military ranks under Batista during the insurrection, Castro decided that the highest rank in the Rebel Army would be that of major. Theoretically, he and his brother, as well as Guevara, were equal in rank to the most obscure major; obviously then, some majors had more power than others. This *de facto* situation was formalized with the 1973 hierarchical reform. The army now has three types of officers, each one with three or four ranks: superior, first, and subaltern. The superior officers' category includes four ranks from "army commander" (four-star general granted only to Commander-in-Chief Fidel Castro) down to "brigade commander" (one-star general). Raúl Castro has become a lieutenant general (two-star general) leaving two ranks vacant between him and his brother. The superior officers' category includes three ranks from colonel to major (formerly the highest rank); and the subaltern officers' category includes four ranks from captain to sublieutenant. The navy also has three categories (including ten ranks), going from admiral to rear admiral, from commodore to commander, and from lieutenant commander to ensign.[31] Explaining the reasons for the new hierarchy, Fidel Castro said that the armed forces had been distinguished in the past for "their modesty in uniform and rank" but that the Revolution had become more mature and so had the armed forces. Other official reasons were the increasing complexity of the armed forces and the need to provide ranks equivalent with those of other countries (e.g., U.S.S.R., Peru) that had a different hierarchy.[32] The new hierarchy has probably been accompanied by salary increases for the top ranks and could be seen also as an economic incentive for the new military elite.

Figures 1 and 2 attempt to illustrate the Cuban politico-administrative system, both as it existed up to the end of the 1960s and as it is developing in the 1970s. Figure 1, however, faces the difficulty of the lack of clear separation of functions among the Council of Ministers, the armed forces, and the Communist party. Figure 2 is faced with the problem that Cuba is in the midst of a process of transformation whose end may be guessed but which is impossible to predict with total accuracy. Thus it is well to keep in mind that these figures are *very tentative;* their purpose is to illustrate the politico-administrative changes that have taken place even though they are in need of further refinement.

The Democratization of the Labor Movement

From 1959 to 1970, the trade union movement went—as an official Cuban publication states—through a period of decline "which almost ended in total dissolution," due to the alleged "total identity between the government and the workers' interest." Economic demands, the crucial activity of the unions before, ceased to be a matter of struggle "because the government was expected to take care of them." The unions were assigned new tasks such as "to win the workers for the Revolution, fight the counterrevolution, and push production forward." But, since these were also government and party tasks, the unions "became ancillary instruments" in the pursuit of such goals. "Trade union democracy was limited and formal . . . it was neither encouraged nor practiced." The absence of institutional channels, such as the holding of periodic meetings, impeded the workers in

FIGURE 1

The Politico-administrative System of Cuba at the End of the 1960s

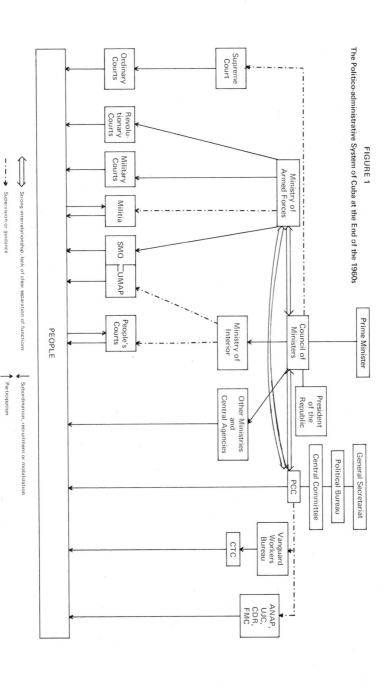

⟺ Strong interrelationship; lack of clear separation of functions

– · – ·→ Supervision or guidance

→ Subordination, recruitment or mobilization

← Participation

FIGURE 2
Trends in the Politico-administrative System of Cuba in the mid-1970s

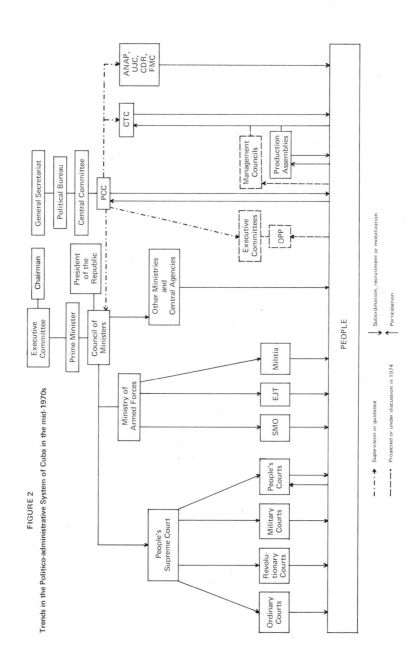

manifesting their opinions. "A common question in the decade of the 1960s was: which is the role of the trade unions? Many thought that the unions could be eliminated without the nation losing anything, because the government, the administration, and the party were apparently capable of doing whatever the unions could do." Beginning in 1967, the problem was aggravated by the launching of the movement of vanguard workers, composed of the most productive and revolutionary workers in an enterprise. "In theory and practice, in many enterprises, the movement [composed by a selected minority] substituted for the union [which embraced the majority of the workers]." Vanguard workers began to decide by themselves, in the name of the workers, on the few things left to the unions.[33]

In May 1970, Castro acknowledged that the trade union movement had been abandoned and that it should be strengthened and democratized. Two months later, Minister of Labor Risquet, in one of the Revolution's most remarkable speeches of self-criticism, said:

> Theoretically, the administrator represents the interest of the worker and peasant state, the interest of all the people. Theory is one thing and practice another. . . . The worker may have a right established by the Revolution [that is not respected or a complaint against the administration] and there is no one to defend him. He does not know where to turn. He turns to the party and it does not know [about the worker's right] or it is busy mobilizing people for production . . . the party is so involved with the management that in many instances it has ceased to play its proper role, has become somewhat insensitive to the problems of the masses. . . . If the party and the administration are one, then there is nowhere the worker can take his problem. . . . The trade union either does not exist or it has become the vanguard workers' bureau. . . .[34]

To correct this situation, Risquet suggested two concrete measures: (1) Elections would be held for the directorate of all the trade union (local) sections in the country. He said that there should not be the slightest fear that conditions would be placed on the election of the representatives and that the elections should be free and open. (2) The unions should be given an opportunity to perform their natural role. Their *first duty* should be to see that labor legislation is applied and workers' rights protected. (Discussion of this point is left for the following section.)[35] In September Castro ratified the first point, announcing: "We are going to trust our workers and hold trade union elections in all locals. . . . They will be absolutely free, and the workers will choose the candidates [and] elect their leaders."[36]

This announcement was followed by meetings of both the National Council and the National Committee of the Confederation of Cuban Workers (CTC), which set the election dates (November 9 through December 9, 1970), enacted the electoral procedures, and defined the composition and functions of the local unions. The elections would be preceded by a general assembly held at the enterprise and attended by all its workers. At these assemblies, any worker could be openly and freely nominated as a candidate regardless of whether or not he was a trade union official. Next the assemblies would discuss the "merits" of the candidates for the job; this discussion would be intended for information only and all candidates would eventually appear on the ballot. There should be at least two or three candidates for each post in order to give voters a good option. The number of posts to be chosen would depend on the size of the enterprise: 3 to 5 in enterprises with 10 to 50 workers, 7 to 9 in those with 51 to 100 workers, and 11 in those with more than 100 workers. An electoral commission, composed of workers, would organize and conduct the election. Voting would be secret; the secretary general of the union would be selected directly by the workers, and the other posts would be distributed among those elected.[37]

The elections took place as announced and were widely publicized. The press reported partial electoral results in early December, but nothing else was said until May Day 1971, when Castro released one single figure on the elections (the number of unions established). Final results were given by Castro one year after. (See table 5.) The table shows that the ratio of candidates to posts was planned to be two or three to one, in the partial results the ratio was about two to one, and in the final results was one-and-a half to one. It seems that in the small enterprises (which were probably reporting late) only one

TABLE 5

Trade Union Elections in Cuba: 1970

	Planned October 1970	Partial Results December 1970	Final Results May 1972
Local sections established	–––––	26,427	37,047
Attendance at candidate-choosing assemblies	2,000,000	887,525	1,244,688
Number of voters		867,373	–––––
Number of candidates	500,000 to 750,000	224,875	262,967
Number of officials elected	250,000	117,625	164,367

Sources: Column 1: "Acuerdos del Comité Nacional de la CTC," *Granma,* October 30, 1972, p. 2, column 2: *Granma,* December 3, 1970, p. 1, column 3: F. Castro, "Speech at the May Day Parade and Workers' Rally," *Granma Weekly Review,* May 7, 1972, p. 2.

candidate appeared on the ballot. Only about half of the expected workers participated in the assemblies to select the candidates, and thousands of workers who attended the assemblies did not vote. The number of officials finally elected was 35 percent below the expected number. The average number of officials elected by each union section was four, a rather low figure when contrasted with the range of from three to eleven officials set by the electoral procedure. Nationwide, some 27 percent of those elected were old union officials, but in Havana about 40 percent of incumbent officials managed to keep their posts.[38]

Were the elections truly free and democratic? According to the official news media, they were. And yet there are some indications that the government used both pressure and manipulation throughout the electoral process. When the CTC was discussing the electoral procedure, strong criticism was voiced by some union members against the traditional methods. This embarrassed the old union leaders, one of whom candidly complained: "We turned the rabbit loose before the hunter had his rifle ready." The Minister of

Labor had to intervene to stop the critics, calling them "counterrevolutionaries" and "demagogues" and warning that such "a negative
situation [had] to be changed radically."[39]

When breaking the news of the elections, Castro had said: "The
[elected official] will have the moral authority of his election, and
when the Revolution establishes a line, he will go all out to defend
and fight for that line."[40] Thus he assumed that only those workers
who would unconditionally follow government, management, and
party orders would be elected. The election was important to
legitimize a behavior typical of the 1960s.

The electoral procedure prohibited candidates from advertising
their candidacy by any means, the electoral commission being the
only one to publicize the candidates' "merits" on bulletin boards and
in murals.[41] The CTC did not set the exact criteria for such merits,
but Castro indirectly stressed revolutionary loyalty and militancy;
hence, it is valid to assume that substantial weight was given by the
commission to such merits. As the table shows, the participation of
workers in the electoral process was below expectations (half of both
the labor force and the government announced figure), perhaps
because they did not expect any real changes or they had one single
candidate to vote for on the ballot.

Most of the new officials (almost three-fourths of those elected)
fulfilled government aspirations (as obviously did the one-fourth of
incumbents who stayed). Those few who did not meet the standard of
loyalty soon came under fire as Minister of Labor Risquet revealed:

> In the great majority of work centers, the masses elected
> their best representatives. . . . There were some cases, how-
> ever—very few of them we must say—where workers elected
> did not have sufficient merits or the merits which would entitle
> them to act as leaders. . . . [Every one of these cases] is a
> danger signal to the trade union movement and to the party,
> pointing out the location or the manifestation of the failures in
> our political work. . . . Each of these "warning lights"
> constitutes a challenge to our political strength, to the power of
> the ideas of the Revolution . . .[42]

At the same time that the elections were taking place in the local unions, a reorganization of the national trade unions began which was not completed until late 1973. In October 1970, the CTC approved rules for the reorganization of the national trade unions. It was to be preceded by national assemblies on production, attended by government, administration, and union representatives, and in which problems of production and productivity would be discussed. Since most national trade unions had been organized prior to the revolutionary takeover (although there were some changes in 1961 and 1966), the trade union structure was not coordinated with the radical transformation of the administrative structure. Thus it was decided that instead of workers being partly organized by trade, all should be in vertical unions parallel to the central ministries and agencies; in other words, all workers employed by a central ministry or agency would be unionized together regardless of their trade. Each national union would be like a pyramid with the ministry or agency at the vertex, then the regional branches, then the consolidated enterprises and the plants (or farms or agencies) at the bottom thus facilitating control of production and productivity.[43]

From November 1970 to September 1973, a total of twenty-three national unions were established: Basic Industry; Mining and Metallurgy; Light Industry; Food; Sugar; Petroleum; Tobacco; Fishing; Agriculture and Cattle Raising; Forestry; News and Book Publishing; Construction; Transportation; Communications; Civil Aviation; Merchant Marine and Ports; Education and Sciences; Hotel and Restaurant; Commerce; Public Health; Public Administration; Civil Employees of the Armed Forces; and Arts and Entertainment. The first national unions established were all those in industry and transportation, plus the armed forces, next followed unions in other productive sectors, then services, and finally agriculture.[44] The unions first organized were those with a relatively small membership, high concentration, discipline, and skills which happened to be in the most strategic sectors (these were organized very fast: eleven in less than one year). Services and agriculture, with large numbers of workers, usually dispersed and less skilled, were slowly organized (it took two years to establish the remaining twelve unions).

The Role of the Unions: Defense of Workers' Rights and Participationism

In the fall of 1970 it was acknowledged that unions were transmission belts of the administration for the implementation of production plans. To correct this situation—it was promised—unions would be allowed to perform their natural role (the defense of workers' rights) and to participate in national decision making and enterprise management. One year later, however, there was no significant change in the official conception of the unions' role, as Raúl Castro stressed:

> [Under capitalism] the trade unions are the instruments that organize and lead the working masses in the struggle for their just demands. . . . However, when the working class is in power the role of the trade unions is changed. . . . There are no antagonisms between the working class and the revolutionary power [the government]. . . . One of the principal functions of the trade unions under socialism is to serve as a vehicle for the orientation, directives, and goals which the revolutionary power must convey to the working masses. . . . The trade unions are [also] the most powerful link between the party and the working masses. That is one of their principal missions. . . . Moreover, the work of the trade unions helps and supports that of the administration. . . . The principal tasks [in which the unions should be involved] are productivity and work discipline; more efficient utilization of the workday; norming and organization; quality, conservation, and most efficient and rational use of both material and human resources.[45]

Unions were also increasingly performing cultural and recreational functions for their membership, such as the organization of vacations (in 1972 a vacation plan for 250,000 workers was announced), education (a campaign is under way to recruit young workers into vocational schools), and recreation (such as the 1972 carnivals).[46]

To the promised "collective bodies" with worker representation to manage state enterprises, Jorge Risquet put stringent limitations:

> The fact that Fidel and I have suggested that the workers should be consulted does not mean that we are going to negate the vanguard role that the Party must play. . . . [There should not be] expectations or hope for magic solutions. . . .[47] The decision and responsibility [in the enterprise] fall to the management, whose job is to take the daily, necessary measures required by the process of production. . . . One thing that is perfectly clear is that the management should have—and does have—all the authority to act. It is charged with a responsibility and it has the authority to make decisions.[48]

In mid-1971, Castro announced that the 13th National Congress of the CTC, to be held at the end of 1972, would debate the issues of union defense of workers' rights and participation in national and enterprise decision making.[49] (The 13th Congress was the first to be held in six years, since 1966, when the 12th Congress of the CTC endorsed the Sino-Guevarist line. The 11th Congress of the CTC, held in 1962, endorsed the Soviet line prevalent at that time. The 10th Congress of the CTC, the first under the Revolution, was held in 1959.) And yet the climate in 1971 was not propitious for such a debate. The brief discussion that preceded the elections in the local unions had been a warning of what could be expected by an uncontrolled membership at a national congress. The "safe" results of such elections provided minimum guarantees for avoiding embarrassing incidents, but the government probably wanted to complete the reorganization of the national unions and have enough time for the preparation of the debate. Thus the congress was postponed for one year, until November of 1973. In the meantime, the remaining reorganization of national unions was finished and the CTC made public nine "theses" for discussion prior to the congress.[50] Although about 88 percent of all workers in the state sector participated in the debate and this took considerable time and energy, the theses set a framework for and put limitations on the scope of the discussion. The following official quotation gives a good picture of the tone of the debate:

> During the discussion [of the theses] every worker who wanted to criticize the administration about concrete aspects of its

work was given a chance to do so. . . . No political, moral, or any other pressures were applied to him. . . . The criticism voiced in the assemblies [however] cannot be viewed as the expression of any antiadministration trend, because, if such were to develop, the CTC would be the first to oppose it. . . . [The kind of criticism expressed was] in line with the role which the trade union movement can and should play.[51]

All the theses were approved by more than 99 percent of the votes, the highest opposing vote against a thesis being 0.2 percent. It has been officially reported that: (1) the voting was done by the public raising of hands; (2) figures for the number of opposition votes were exact because there were only a few of them and hence the accounting—and obviously the identification of the worker—was easy; and (3) there was no attempt to demand the inclusion of issues which were not within the framework of the theses.[52]

The 13th Congress approved twenty-one resolutions which did not always coincide with the theses. Some of the latter were not subjects of resolutions, others were modified by them, and there were resolutions in areas not tackled by the theses. As secretary general of the CTC, the congress selected Lázaro Peña, an old member of the PSP. (Peña was one of the founders of the CTC back in 1939 and its first secretary general in 1939–1947 mostly under the Popular Front of the PSP with Batista. He almost vanished from public life in the next fifteen years. Well trusted by the U.S.S.R., at the 11th Congress of the CTC in 1962 he was elected by single ballot as Secretary General of the CTC and remained in the job until Cuban-Soviet relations deteriorated in 1966. A sexagenarian, Peña returned to public activities in 1970, became involved in the reorganization of the unions, and was elected by 99 percent of the vote in the 13th Congress of the CTC as its Secretary General for 1973–1977. He died in March 1974, after having served four months in office.) In the rest of this section, it is explained how the theses for and the resolutions of the 13th Congress dealt with the issues of union defense of workers' rights, participation in national decision making, and in enterprise management.

The theses did not include any innovation on the subject of union defense of workers' rights. According to the theses, there are no conflicts but cooperation among the state administration, the party, and the unions because they share the same goal: "Always producing more and better." The congress approved new statutes and declarations of principles for the Cuban labor movement, in substitution of those enacted in the 1966 congress. The new principles state that unions are autonomous bodies which are neither part of the state apparatus nor of the party but that they are politically guided and directed by the party and must follow its policies. The objectives of the unions, as listed in the statutes, did not differ from those prevalent in 1966–1970 or as summarized by Raúl Castro in 1971. The general objectives are: support the revolutionary government, participate in national vigilance and defense activities, cooperate to improve managerial performance, strengthen labor discipline and fight any violations of it, and raise the political consciousness of their affiliates. More concrete objectives are to promote punctual daily attendance at work; maximum utilization of the workday; increases of output, productivity, and quality; saving raw materials and energy; adequate maintenance of the equipment; inventions to improve production; and development of cultural, recreational, and sports activities. The document also generally said that the unions should protect workers' rights, check the enforcement of labor legislation and safety measures, and assist affiliates who have complaints.[53]

Only one form of union participation in national decisions was endorsed by the theses: evaluation in public discussion of legal drafts on significant labor issues. This was a common practice in the 1960s and early 1970s, particularly when sensitive legislation had to be enacted (e.g., the law against loafing). In practice, the law eventually passed was a replica of the draft, suggesting that the labor movement did not have real power to modify it. The theses recommended various innovations to correct that situation: (1) the draft should be distributed with enough anticipation and accompanied by explanatory materials in simple language; (2) all opinions voiced either for or against the draft, or suggesting its modification, should be heard; and (3) suitable suggestions arising from public discussion should be incorporated in the law and an official explanation given when such suggestions are rejected. In his main report to the Congress, Secretary General Peña requested more direct participation of the unions in social security administration, setting price policies, and distribution of certain goods.[54] In his speech closing the Congress, Castro suggested that a representation from the CTC should be invited to the meetings of the Executive Committee of the Council of Ministers where plans and other crucial administrative decisions are made.[55] At the beginning of the spring of 1974 no measures had been taken—at least publicly—to implement Peña's and Castro's suggestions.

The theses prescribed that unions should participate in the administration of the enterprise through two institutions: "production assemblies" and "management councils." The assemblies are not new and have not changed their aims; they were common in the 1960s and, in 1971, the Minister of Labor described their functions as follows: "[Unions must] make every effort to get all the workers into the assemblies, [make them] approve and consider as their own the production plans or whatever activity is involved, [and turn the assemblies] into the tool that will make it possible for us to attain, day after day, [a high] degree of mobilization, interest, and enthusiasm behind the production goals."[56] The objectives of the new assemblies were listed by the theses: fulfilling and overfulfilling production plans, tightening labor discipline, increasing productivity, using resources more rationally, and improving the quality of the product or service. Prior to the congress, the assemblies could make recommendations to the manager concerning production problems and their potential solutions, but the follow-up procedure was not specified. The theses give the manager the option to implement or reject the assembly's recommendation according to his judgment, but he had to explain the reasons for rejection in the next assembly or the results of the adoption of a recommendation. No sanctions were regulated for the manager who failed to fulfill his obligations with the assembly. The brief resolution on production assemblies passed by the congress did not enter into any of the details contained in the theses, but only set the overall goals of the assemblies and requested from the government the enactment of a law regulating their functions.[57] Concerning "management councils," the theses recommended that union representatives should participate in them but did not determine the number of such representatives, procedure for their selection, or concrete functions. According to the theses, the councils' function was to approve or make suggestions to modify production plans prepared by the manager following "directives issued by the state." The councils were also to be "informed" of any change in the production plan decided by the manager. There was no resolution passed by the congress on this matter.

Nothing can be said on the implementation of the recommendations of the CTC Congress because only a few months had elapsed between their approval and the conclusion of this book. Basically, the *first duties* of the unions in the 1973 statutes are exactly those listed in the statutes of 1966 and in those of 1961: to cooperate with the state, the party, and the enterprise manager in improving production and efficiency. Less emphasized functions are to promote cultural and recreational facilities and to defend the workers' rights. The "new" participatory power of the unions is small and essentially related to production; unions do not intervene in the determination of salaries, hiring or dismissal of managers, or investment plans. Certainly the degree of participation allowed on paper fell far behind the expectations of 1970, and yet, if such power is implemented, the unions would be strengthened. It should be recalled, nevertheless, that this is not the first time that the Cuban government has approved and later dropped a plan for labor or mass participation in decision making.

In 1960–1962 "technical advisory councils" were set up in enterprises, candidates from the workers were selected, the councils' functions were carefully regulated, and the matter then shelved. In 1966, the creation of the so-called *Poder Local* was announced. Both rural and urban municipalities would be represented in local governing councils through which the people could articulate the needs of the community. In 1967, some 22,000 delegates were elected. But the councils were suspended indefinitely in 1968, and new elections for delegates scheduled for 1969 were cancelled.[58] In 1970 Castro promised the creation of city-district bodies integrated by representatives of mass organizations to closely supervise, at the local level, the state administration and the party. For almost four years nothing was said about these bodies, until early 1974 when Raúl Castro presented a watered-down version of them. He announced that from mid-1974 to mid-1975 a pilot project would be tested in Matanzas province to later set up nationally "organs of popular power" (OPP). These organs, integrated by "non-professional delegates elected and subjected to recall by the masses" would promote mass participation in "state and administrative affairs" in an institutionalized manner.[59] In May 1974 two significant amendments to the constitution (Ley Fundamental of 1959) were passed. One granted all Cuban citizens sixteen years of age and over (including members of the armed forces) the right to vote by secret ballot. The other law introduced a commission to regulate and conduct the election, establishment, and functioning of executive committees of the OPP (at the municipal, regional, and provincial levels) in the province of Matanzas. The OPP's functions, as enumerated in the law are: to govern and administer economic institutions in the production and services fields, do construction and repair work, and in general carry out activities to meet the economic social, educational, cultural, and recreational needs of the . . . area."[60] Blas Roca was appointed head of the commission and there are indications that the PCC will guide the OPPs. The latter strongly resemble the U.S.S.R.'s "organs of people's power" or "Soviets."[61]

The future will show whether the "management councils," the "organs for popular power," and other announced participatory forms will materialize and take roots or follow the path of their forgotten predecessors.

A final comment is due on a series of measures taken since 1970—parallel with the reorganization of the unions—which seem to indicate a trend of governmental tightening of control over the workers. In September 1970, Minister of Labor Risquet referred to two steps that had already been taken to insure adequate control over the labor force: the elimination of the nonagricultural private sector (to expand state control over employment and avoid simulation of work); and the taking of a national population and housing census (to measure the size of the labor force and its distribution by occupation and location).[62] Measures to be discussed in this section are: the launching of a campaign to make managers more demanding of workers, the improvement of the system of worker's identity cards and labor records, the reestablishment of work quotas to measure output and productivity, the enactment of a law against loafing to curtail labor absenteeism and integrate loafers into the labor force, and the introduction of collective work commitments.

The campaign to make managers more demanding of their employees was a constant in the production assemblies held in 1971. In October, the Sixth Council of the CTC exhorted management "to strengthen itself [so] its standards of conduct should be one of demand rather than spiritlessness." At the Council, Castro denounced managers who lacked "the character to make demands" as "one of the worst ills of the Revolution." The Minister of Labor, in turn, condemned "the demagogic manager, the politickers, and the characters who go around doing little favors" for the workers, and added: "We must reaffirm the role of the manager . . . in demanding that the workers come to work every day; that they make the most efficient use of the workday; that they comply with the established norms with regard to quantity and quality; that the equipment be kept in perfect working order; that no material is wasted; and that every possible measure which will contribute to consolidate work discipline be adopted."[63] By the end of 1971, an editorial of the party's newspaper *Granma* admonished the workers to be demanding of their own comrades, warning that those "who shut their eyes to sloppy work just because they don't want to look for trouble are committing acts of complicity and have an attitude unworthy of the working class." *Granma* exhorted the workers to "fight against this attitude and eliminate it from our industries and work centers."[64]

Each worker employed by the state (probably 90 percent of the labor force) has to have an identification card to get a job and a file with a complete record of his merits and "demerits" (faults). The merits include, among other things: voluntary (unpaid) labor in the sugar crop; overfulfillment of work quotas; overtime work without pay; postponement of retirement to continue working; defense of socialist (state) property; and a high level of political consciousness. Demerits (defined as "activities that negatively affect production, disturb labor discipline, and show a low level of consciousness") to be included in the file are, among others: absenteeism; negligence in handling equipment, raw materials, and fuel; nonfulfillment of work quotas; abandonment of the work in the enterprise without previous authorization; and deserting labor camps before completing the term to which the worker has committed himself. The "file" also registers any sanction applied to the worker by civil, military, revolutionary, and people's courts.[65]

As it has been explained in chapter 2, work quotas were first introduced and applied in Cuba in 1963–1965, neglected in 1966–1970 (when Sino-Guevarism was in vogue), and refixed and reinforced since mid–1970. Each worker is assigned a quota which determines how much should be produced by him at a given work schedule. Managerial control of fulfillment of the quotas (as well as exhortation for overfulfillment and sanctions for underfulfillment) is basic for enterprise productivity. As we have already seen, the labor file also registers the worker's performance in this matter.

In the spring of 1971, the government enacted a law against loafing which established the obligation of working upon all men from ages seventeen through sixty, who are physically and mentally capable. One of the main purposes of the law was to incorporate idle men into production, and more than 100,000 were indeed recruited even before the law went into force. Another objective was to curtail the increasing absenteeism of the labor force which reached some 20 percent by late 1970. Absentees for more than fifteen days are in a "precriminal stage of loafing" while recurrent absentees commit a "crime of loafing." Penalties fluctuate from house arrest to imprisonment in a rehabilitation center at forced labor for a period ranging from one to two years.[66] The CTC gave full endorsement to the law against loafing.[67] Since the enactment of the law, four national meetings have taken place to check the work done by the courts. In a National Council of the CTC held in late 1971, Minister Risquet reported violations of the law, criticized managers who did not report absentee workers, and exhorted the strict enforcement of the law.[68] In a National Plenary Meeting on Labor Justice held at the beginning of 1972, some fifty recommendations were made (but not published) to improve management enforcement of the law, workers' cooperation in strengthening labor discipline, the courts' application of the law, and the behavior of those loafers incorporated into the labor force.[69]

The 13th Congress of the CTC approved the introduction of "collective work commitments" between the enterprise management and the workers and their unions. Quantified commitments are made by the workers concerning the fulfillment and overfulfillment of daily, monthly, and annual work quotas; the savings of raw materials and energy; and the donation of unpaid labor. The workers also commit themselves to avoid absenteeism, tardiness, and any other violation of labor discipline. The union should use "persuasion in order that all workers make commitments in all the various aspects." The administration and the union join in keeping careful control of the commitments. Monthly and annual assemblies discuss the worker's fulfillment of his commitments in front of his job comrades and the results are put in a visible place in the work center.[70]

Restructuration of Mass Organizations: The Small Farmers

Soon after Batista's ouster, the revolutionary leadership faced a crucial decision: whether to distribute the increasingly nationalized latifundia among the mass of landless rural wage workers that cultivated it or to keep it undivided.[71] The prevalent opinion (materialized in the 1959 agrarian reform) was to give away the ownership of land already divided into plots and held by sharecroppers, tenant farmers, and squatters, but against dividing the latifundia and converting the rural wage earners into private, independent farmers. The government's alleged reasons against this were of an ideological, political, and economic nature (that is, to impede a regression in the matter of ownership, to keep control over agriculture and the rural workers, and to avoid decline in productivity resulting from parcelization). The latifundia (mainly sugar plantations and cattle ranches) were briefly organized as pseudo-cooperatives which, by mid–1962, were transformed into state farms. One year later, the second agrarian reform eliminated the middle-sized independent farmer (the Cuban "kulak"). Although the resistance of private farmers in Cuba cannot be compared with that of the kulaks in the U.S.S.R., there were bloody clashes in the early 1960s between Escambray farmers who went to the mountains and state troops trained in guerrilla warfare.

At the end of 1966, there were some 234,000 small private farmers who controlled about 35 percent of the arable land. They were, however, incorporated into the National Association of Small Farmers (ANAP), which, in turn, was integrated into the national agricultural plans and supervised by INRA. Private farmers had to resort to government agencies for their supply of seed, fertilizer, tools, and credit, and to sell part of their crops to the state *(acopio)* at prices officially set below the market price. The size of the private sector was further reduced in 1967–1971 (to 203,000 farmers and 32 percent of the arable land) through government purchases of some 10,000 farms and through the retirement and death of owners (ownership of land is not hereditary).[72] Furthermore, the size of the *acopio* was substantially expanded to embrace in some areas the total crop (e.g., the Havana "Green Belt"). In these cases the government paid "rent" to the farmer and allowed him to use a small plot of the farm for his own consumption. Until 1968, the small surplus of agricultural production (that part neither sold to the state nor consumed by the farmer and his family) was mostly sold at very high prices to urbanites who used it for their own consumption, transformation into other goods or services, or sale on the black market. During the "Revolutionary Offensive" of 1968 the government drastically curtailed these activites, hence reducing the marketability of the surplus. Small farmers still do some cash selling in very small quantities but mainly barter for other products that they need.

Most rural workers became state employees in 1962 when the cooperatives were transformed into state farms. Some of them, however, were hired by the private farms which began to flourish in spite of governmental restrictions. But gradually the government managed to reduce the number of these private wage earners from about 150,000 in 1962 to from 30,000 to 60,000 in 1966. This trend was accelerated in 1971 when, after passage of the law against loafing, the ANAP launched a campaign to detect and transfer to the state sector thousands of idle men partly employed on private farms, or working full time on them but at "low productivity."[73] The rural wage workers employed on state farms were allowed small family plots for their families' use and consumption. These plots were eliminated in 1967 under the allegation that the workers were giving more time to family plots than to the state land. A good number of rural workers (estimated at 6 to 10 percent of the total labor force) have been reluctant to become unionized and hold conservative views. In 1972, the CTC launched a campaign to incorporate some 150,000 of these rural workers into its membership.[74]

By the end of 1971, the Fourth Congress of the ANAP was held as part of the "new phase" of the Revolution and the reorganization of mass organizations. The complete record of the Congress is not available (only Castro's closing speech was published in the press and the final resolutions transmitted on the radio). But it appears that there was at the Congress a heated debate between the state administration and private farmers and between the latter and the workers employed on state farms. According to Castro, both the state administration and state-farm workers "made quite serious accusations" against the private farmers who "got the worst of it." The prime minister sided in favor of the state and against some of the "incredible" things requested by the private farmers: "Sometimes one must resort to rawness if one is to put a message across."[75] The four main resolutions approved by the Congress reveal the main points of friction that arose and how the position of the private farmer was weakened by the Congress.[76]

The first resolution exhorted the progressive incorporation of the private farms and their labor force into the state sector, with the objective of eradicating "every vestige left of class and private ownership of the means of production." (In spite of the government's efforts to accelerate such incorporation, by the end of 1971 only 50,556 farmers, equivalent to 25 percent of the total, had been incorporated.[77]) The resolution claimed that such incorporation would occur in a voluntary manner, without the use of force, violence, or coercion, but the ANAP is committed to the use of political education to convince the farmers of its advantages.

Another resolution dealt with the selling of agricultural surplus and the battle against the black market. Some small farmers requested that the Congress annul Law No. 1035, which punishes the illegal traffic of agricultural products. The Congress rejected the request, and Castro advised how to treat those farmers who would not accept the decision: "Those individuals who engage in black market operations should be made the object of political work. And the incorrigible ones should be deprived of all their rights [and] be treated as a class enemy."[78]

Two important resolutions dealt with the private farmers who are totally integrated into the *acopio* system. The Congress decided that the "rent" paid to these farmers should not cover all their necessities in order that these farmers work part time on state land. Eventually the time devoted to the state should become the main source of the farmers' income "because in a nation of workers it would be illogical to develop a social class of rentists." The Congress also showed concern about the small plots allowed to these farmers for family consumption. Although the plot was not abolished, the Congress stated that in the future the plot should disappear and the farmer devote all his time to the state land.

In summary, the private farmer who is not fully integrated into the *acopio* as yet is under political pressure to take that step in a voluntary manner. His incentive to generate a surplus for marketing is greatly reduced due to the stricter enforcement of sanctions against illegal traffic of agricultural products. On the other hand, the fully integrated private farmer should gradually yield his "rent" and reduce his work on the family plot in order to work more and more for the state land. The fate of the only private or quasi-private sector left in Cuba is clear: total absorption by the state sector.

Restructuration of Mass Organizations: The Youth

As part of the process of strengthening mass organizations, it was publicly acknowledged in 1970 that the work with the youth had been abandoned with grave negative consequences of a political, educational, and moral nature. Thus among the youth there was "a backward minority made up of those who neither study nor work, or do so only under pressure—those who, permeated by the old ideology which still remains at the bottom of certain strata of our society, maintain a conduct which is contrary to socialist morals."[79]

The Secretary General of the Young Communist League (UJC), Jaime Crombet, said that this association, founded in 1962, had a "poor, rachitic membership" a decade later—120,000 members out of more than two million youngsters.[80] Due to the poor political work of the UJC, the objective of raising the consciousness and self-discipline of the youth could not be achieved and this failure affected, in turn, other areas such as education.

In spite of the remarkable progress by the Cuban Revolution in education (e.g., reduction of the illiteracy rate from 23 to 4 or 5 percent; doubling the number of elementary schools, student registration, personnel, and graduates; increasing the proportion of children of school age in school from 56 to 98 percent) serious deficiencies were reported. In April 1971, out of the total number of school-age youngsters (4 to 16) there were 300,000 who neither studied nor worked. Apparently the law against loafing reduced this figure to 215,513 one year after. This figure was equivalent to only 12 percent of the total student population, but the percentage dramatically increased with age (e.g., 23 percent among those 14 years old, 44 percent among those 15, and 60 percent among those 16). The dropout rate was very high: in elementary schools, 79 percent of those who entered the class of 1965 did not finish in 1971. The dropout rate was worse in rural areas (88 percent) than in urban schools (66 percent). The rate of dropout in junior high school was higher than in elementary school (86 percent).

Some of the official reasons given to explain this phenomenon were of a material nature: poor school installations, difficult accessibility of schools, and deficient training of teachers (in elementary schools only 39 percent of the teachers had finished their studies, while in junior high only 27 percent had finished). But it was also reported that the students did not show enough enthusiasm, perhaps because they were spoiled: "Before it was papa who paid all the expenses for the student and, afterwards, it was the state. A lot of revolutionary talk, a lot of political indoctrination but, in the end, that man is not simply abstract ideas. The university will never educate a man more than a factory will."[81] The lack of systematic, constant, daily work and discipline among students was acknowledged by Castro: "Scholarship students and students in general are willing to do anything, except to study hard."[82]

The emphasis placed and the great efforts made by the Revolution to attract young farmers and workers into vocational and technological schools (especially agricultural ones) was crowned by success in the mid–1960s. But later the number of students registered at those schools declined dramatically and, in 1972, some were empty. In 1971, there were 24,033 students in language schools, but 16,203 in industrial schools and only 7,757 in agricultural schools. Castro explained that the idea of moral motivation had failed and there was a lack of material incentives: "Who wants to go to work in the countryside? [It] is rough, it is poor . . . it doesn't change from one year to the next [and will stay like it is] for years to come."[83]

Students also showed a lack of concern for and responsibility with socialist property. According to the Minister of Education, 50 percent of the books sent to schools were lost every year due to lack of care. Castro exploded in indignation: "There's something wrong when we have to educate our young people in the need to care for socialist property. . . . Loafers, people who don't work, criminals are the ones who destroy."[84]

Youngsters wore "extravagant foreign fashions" (too-short miniskirts in the case of girls; and the boys, too-tight pants and long hair), listened to American music, and liked "decadent" literature. In some cases these youngsters "were used by counterrevolutionaries in protests against the Revolution." It was also reported that "residual manifestations" of prostitution and homosexuality were found among the youth.[85] In 1967, minors had participated in 41 percent of crimes of all types committed in the nation; four years later the percentage had risen to 50 percent.[86]

There were also rumors about an incident that occurred in October 1970 at the University of Oriente in Santiago de Cuba. Apparently at a student assembly, four or five attendants criticized governmental policies and accused Castro of being an autocrat. Two days later the prime minister visited the campus, called a meeting, and engaged in a heated dialogue with one of his critics. After Castro left, another student assembly expelled all the students who had voiced criticism.[87]

To analyze the roots of the problems mentioned above and take measures to cope with them, two national meetings were held in Havana: the First National Congress on Education and Culture in April 1971, and the Second Congress of the UJC in April 1972. The UJC Congress detected a "serious weakness" in the previous political work of this organization and launched a campaign to recruit the hundreds of thousands of youngsters outside of it or at least to exert political influence upon them. (The campaign apparently was successful because in March 1974 an increase of 62 percent in the UJC membership was announced.) The UJC Congress also decided to raise the low political level of its cadres and militant members. Top priority was given by the UJC to children, recognizing that childhood is a crucial period for the future development of communist ideology. The political work of the UJC should be extended "to make every young person a self-sacrificing fighter" for increased production and productivity, reduction of production costs, careful use of material resources, and donation of overtime work when necessary. It was also agreed to work closely with the Minister of Education to reduce the dropout rate and direct the students to the fields in which they are most needed. The youth organization requested that "strict, revolutionary measures be taken in the shortest possible time" against youngsters who had antisocial behavior, especially those who neither worked nor studied, and those who were careless, negligent, and irresponsible in handling socialist property.[88]

Concrete measures were suggested by Castro in his speech closing the UJC Congress. The dropout problem could be partially solved through the Compulsory Military Service (SMO) and the "Youth Centennial Column." The SMO recruits—in a three-year period— about one-third of all youngsters ages sixteen to seventeen, some 100,000 annually, for a regular force of 300,000 in 1972. Until 1973, most SMO recruits were integrated into the "Military Units to Aid Production" (UMAP). They worked in agriculture (mainly in the cane fields) and were trained in military discipline and some in a trade. The Column was formed in 1968 recruiting some 40,000 youngsters and in 1972 recruited about 55,000. It was integrated by militarized brigades which worked in construction, irrigation, and other projects. Originally the Column was intended as a one-year experiment, but later it was expected that it would continue until 1980. To cope with the remaining youngsters, compulsory education was to be extended after the sixth grade to cover the age bracket (thirteen to seventeen) with the highest dropout incidence. These youngsters would be subject to special internment combining work and study.[89] Three laws enacted in mid-1973 implemented some of Castro's suggestions through the following regulations: (1) the UMAP and the Column (together with other labor squads) were merged into the "Youth Army of Work" (EJT), a paramilitary body, dependent on the Ministry of Armed Forces, which is devoted to agricultural work (especially in the sugar harvest) and other "shock tasks"; (2) a new "Social Service" program (SS) was made mandatory for graduates who have not served in the SMO or the Column, these graduates having to serve three years working in rural areas; and (3) those who have neither been drafted into SMO nor served in the SS will be assigned for three years to the EJT.[90] As a result of these measures, the dropout rate (especially in high school) declined sharply in 1973. Nevertheless in April 1974 it was reported that the number of youngsters in the 13–16 age bracket who did not study remained practically unchanged.[91]

The Congress on Education recommended eradicating "extravagant foreign fashions, customs, and behavior" and impeding "rebellious groups from bourgeois societies" from becoming examples for Cuban youth. "Maladjusted minors" who commit offenses or have "antisocial behavior" should be interned in school workshops.[92] Two months later Castro alleged that the cause of the high rate of juvenile delinquency was that the youngsters were exempted from criminal sanctions (the prerevolutionary criminal code provided for special treatment of youngsters under eighteen) and suggested a reduction in the age of legal liability.[93] Following the prime minister's recommendation, in May 1973 the age of legal liability was reduced to sixteen years. In addition, tough sanctions (up to life) were introduced for crimes against the national economy, abnormal sexual behavior, and other offenses.[94]

Probably to avoid any repetition of rebellion among the students, the Secretary of Organization of the party announced at the University of Havana in mid-1971 the establishment of "standards for the political evaluation of both new and old students who lack the necessary and moral conditions" and stated that "the right to a university education is a right of revolutionaries only."[95]

In late 1972 an American journalist sympathetic to the Revolution asked a Cuban official why boys were not allowed to wear long hair. The official said that if one boy were allowed to be different in hair (or in dress or behavior) the rest might request the right to be different also. This in turn would create controversy, something that was considered incorrect.[96]

The Congress on Education and Culture and the Intellectuals

In the first decade of the Revolution, there was a remarkable improvement of material facilities for cultural expansion. The number of published books and journals increased four or five times; substantial state support was given to the national theater, cinema arts, and the national ballet; an excellent center for plastic arts and dancing was built; national and international literary contests were generously funded; and most writers and artists were well remunerated or subsidized. But the abolition of royalties; the nationalization of film companies, theaters, publishing houses, magazines, and newspapers; the centralization of cultural, publishing, and film activities under state agencies (respectively the National Council of Culture, the Book Institute, and ICAIC [Cuban Institute of Cinema Arts]); and the unionization of all writers and artists under the state-sponsored National Union of Writers and Artists of Cuba (UNEAC) made the writer and artist totally dependent on the state. The latter used this power to manipulate these intellectuals by hiring or dismissing them from jobs; facilitating, obstructing, or banning publication of their works, exhibition of their films, or staging of their plays; opening and closing publishing houses and journals; pressing the writers and artists to assume a revolutionary attitude in their works by appraisal and criticism through the news media; and rewarding them with national awards and travel abroad, or punishing them with internment in labor camps.

The government position vis-a-vis the intellectuals had been vaguely defined by Castro in 1961: "Inside the Revolution everything; against it nothing." Until 1968, all those who cautiously stayed within these limits were tolerated by the government, although the peace was interrupted by frequent controversies. However, during the Revolutionary Offensive both the government and the UNEAC bitterly criticized two Cuban writers who had been awarded prizes in a literary contest presided over by a jury which included foreign intellectuals. The writers were the poet Heberto Padilla and the playwright Antón Arrufat; both had proclaimed themselves revolutionaries but the government alleged that their works concealed criticism of the authoritarian nature of the regime. This incident was followed in 1969 by an attempt to select militant juries for international literary contests which would award prizes to revolutionary works, and by the expulsion from UNEAC of one writer accused of counterrevolutionary activities.[97] At the end of 1970, Castro expressed concern over "deviations in cultural activities" and announced that a Congress on Education and Culture—which he wanted to take place immediately but that had to be postponed until April 1971—would be the forum to discuss such problems.[98]

Before the Congress began, a series of grave events occurred. In early February, a technician employed by the Cuban government, Raúl Alonso Olivé, who had been assigned as an assistant to Dumont while he was visiting Cuba in 1969, was accused of espionage and sent to prison. The charge against Olivé was that he had handed Dumont a list of black-market prices based on a survey that he had conducted.[99] On March 20, the poet Padilla was jailed. The news filtered abroad and on April 9, a large group of European and Latin American leftist intellectuals (among them Jean Paul Sartre, Gabriel García Márquez, Carlos Fuentes, Octavio Paz, and Mario Vargas Llosa) addressed a letter to Castro expressing concern over Padilla's imprisonment and "the use of repressive methods against intellectuals and writers who exercise the right of criticism."[100] Ten days later Castro indirectly answered: "There are some gentlemen who aspire to intellectual tutelage and cultural colonialism . . . who want to teach our people from such places as New York, Paris, Rome, London, and West Berlin . . . our people must give a resounding call against . . . that inadmissible attempt to introduce and maintain [here] manifestations of a decadent culture, the fruit of societies that are rotten to the core."[101]

While the Congress was in session, Castro attacked the "neocolonializing elements in the [Cuban] cultural movement" who had accepted "foreign cultural impositions" and developed a "snobbish, servile copy of decadent art."[102] Padilla was released on April 25 after handing a confession to the Ministry of Interior. Two days later, and three days before the closing session of the Congress, Padilla read a letter of self-criticism to one hundred writers and artists gathered at the UNEAC headquarters. In this letter he admitted all his "errors against the Revolution," accused Dumont and Karol of being CIA agents, disclosed his links with several signers of the letter to Castro, and denounced the "errors" of four Cuban writers who were present at the meeting (one was his wife, the other three intimate friends of his). Three of the accused stood up, accepted their faults, and asked forgiveness; the only one who tried to defend himself from the accusation, alleging that it was false, was strongly criticized later by a UNEAC official.[103]

In this spiraling climate of tension, the Congress on April 30 passed its final declaration which introduced a tougher line on cultural affairs. In the future it would not be enough for writers and artists to proclaim themselves revolutionaries and to abstain from criticizing the regime; they would also have to prove their militancy by producing political works: "Culture like education is not and cannot be apolitical or impartial. Apoliticism is nothing more than a reactionary and shamefaced attitude in the cultural field. Art is a weapon of the Revolution, a weapon against the penetration of the enemy." In the declaration it was stated that the mass media "are powerful instruments of ideological education whose utilization and development should not be left to spontaneity and improvisation." Control of the mass media should not be dispersed among various state agencies but centralized under "a single politico-cultural leadership." In staffing mass media, as well as universities and artistic institutions, "political and ideological conditions should be taken into account." The declaration also recommended a revision of the regulations of literary contests in order to check the revolutionary credentials of the juries and select the most revolutionary works. The declaration dealt with "foreign influences" in several passages: (1) condemning the Latin American writers who "took refuge in the capitals of the rotten and decadent societies of Western Europe and the United States to become agents of the metropolitan imperialist culture" (a clear reference to those Latin Americans who had signed the letter of protest to Castro); (2) warning that "many pseudorevolutionary writers, who in West Europe masquerade as leftists but in reality uphold positions against socialism, would be unmasked" (this was directed against Dumont and Karol); (3) combatting the possible infiltration of "imperialist cinema, television, and art"; and (4) requesting the establishment of a "strict system" for inviting foreign writers and intellectuals to avoid the presence of persons whose work and ideology does not fit into those of the Revolution.[104]

All of these suggestions were immediately accepted by Castro in his closing speech of the Congress. He said that criteria for and priorities on publications would be imposed upon the Book Institute: "There are privileged minorities writing things of no use, expressions of decadence. . . . Sometimes certain books have been printed [an obvious reference to Padilla's book of poems published in 1968] of which not a single copy, chapter, nor page should be published, not even a letter! . . . Our magazines will be only open to revolutionary writers." Then Castro set the rules for future literary contests: "In order for anybody to act as a member of a jury [or] to win an award, whether national or international, he must be a true revolutionary," that is, a revolutionary "without doubt, hesitation, or half-way measures." Finally Castro informed the "European pseudo-leftists" and the "shameless Latin Americans" that they will never again be jury members or guests of the Cuban government: "Now you know it, bourgeois intellectuals, agents of the CIA, and espionage services of imperialism: you will not be allowed to come to Cuba! Our doors will remain closed indefinitely!"[105]

On May 20, sixty European and Latin American writers, film-makers, and artists answered Castro in a second letter. They stated that Padilla's confession could have been obtained only through torture, and that this recalled "the most sordid moments of Stalinism," with its "dogmatic obscurantism," "cultural xenophobia," and "repressive system."[106] A week later Padilla released a statement saying that his confession was delivered completely voluntarily. (However, in his address to UNEAC he had shrewdly referred to the numerous sessions that he had held for more than a month with MININ [Ministry of Interior] officials whom he finally learned to "admire and love.") Almost at the same time, in a speech commemorating the tenth anniversary of the creation of MININ, Castro defended the integrity of the state security officials and indignantly repudiated "those miserable elements that in the international scene have said that the self-critical statement of a writer who held a counterrevolutionary position came as a result of physical torture." And then Castro acknowledged that the Revolution was under attack from "communist, socialist, Marxist, and leftist positions."[107]

That summer several American scholars, Marxists, or leftists, many of whom had visited Cuba before and were expected to return, found their visas cancelled or never received the expected visas from Cuba.[108] In the fall, a journalist who managed to enter Cuba reported the case of another writer who had been in trouble and lost his job, but transmitted the impression (received from interviews with state officials and writers) that the purge would not continue because the intellectuals had received the message and the government wanted to curb the bad publicity abroad.[109] Nevertheless, the American specialist on Caribbean affairs, Frank McDonald, who had spent two months in Cuba in 1970, returned in May 1971 as a guest lecturer at the University of Havana and published sympathetic reports on the Revolution, was arrested on Christmas eve of 1971. Accused of being a spy (a charge punishable by thirty years in prison or death), McDonald was held incommunicado for three months and frequently subjected to the interrogations of state-security officials. He was finally released because of "lack of evidence" but was deported and his notes confiscated under the allegation that he had gathered "sensitive socioeconomic information" for a book, thus violating a "freeze" imposed by the Cuban government in such studies.[110]

The tide of the ideological campaign did not recede in 1973. The Cuban press attacked "sociological research" conducted in Latin America by U.S. scholars sponsored by such institutions as the Ford Foundation, presenting such activities as espionage, and denouncing an increase of U.S. "cultural penetration" in this area.[111] An American political scientist who in the 1960s had visited Cuba several times and written sympathetic studies of the Revolution was refused a visa by the Cuban government because of his connections with Ford. Two U.S. specialists on the Cuban patriot and litterateur, José Martí, both of whom had also been in Cuba several times, were attacked by the Cuban magazine *El Caimán Barbudo* ("The Bearded Crocodile") because in their works they presented a fragmented view of Martí which neglected his antiimperialist views, while both had received Ford support for a seminar and an institute on Martí.[112] The Cuban government also prohibited radio stations from transmitting U.S. and British pop and folk music (including protest songs) alleging that these caused alienation among the youth.[113]

Democratic versus Centralist-Dogmatic Institutionalization

The changes introduced in 1970–1974 in the Cuban political structure suggest that a process of institutionalization is taking place highlighted by the following nine features:

1. Depersonalization of the government through delegation of power from the prime minister. There seems to be a substitution of the charismatic-personalistic regime prevalent in the 1960s by a technocratic-bureaucratic administration closely resembling that of the Soviet Union.

2. Separation of functions of the central administration, the party, and the army. These three institutions were controlled in the 1960s by Castro and his inner circle, resulting in the absence of delimitation of their functions. Now there is a clear tendency to separate these institutions and assign specific functions to each of them.

3. Concentration in the Council of Ministers of executive and

legislative-constitutional functions and control over the judicial functions. The Council is coordinated by a new Executive Committee integrated by ten deputy prime ministers, (posts typical of the Soviet administration) each one in charge of a sector of the administration.

4. Building up the formerly stagnant Communist party (PCC) so that it will efficiently perform the political-guidance function. The membership of the PCC is being expanded and indoctrinated and the first party congress, scheduled for 1975, is expected to approve the PCC statutes and program and elect all its officials.

5. Concentration of military functions in, and specialization and hierarchicalization of the armed forces. The latter have absorbed the militia and set a timetable for its demise. The armed forces have been reduced in size and centered on strictly military functions, while the productive activities they used to perform are now entrusted to a separate body. The military ranks have been reorganized abandoning the modesty in ranks that was characteristic in the 1960s, and resembling now the complex hierarchy of the Soviet military.

6. Revival and strengthening of the trade unions but within the Soviet concept of transmission belts of the administration. The labor movement has been revitalized through elections in local units, reorganization of national unions, and a national congress of the CTC. In spite of the 1970 rhetoric, however, the unions' primary objective continues to be cooperation with the administration in productive tasks instead of defense of the workers' interests. The promised participation of the unions in enterprise management has been limited to production issues and the really new participatory functions have still to be regulated and implemented. The current statutes of the CTC assert that the unions are not part of the state apparatus (although they have to follow the party's policy) but there are indications that they remain controlled by the administration, e.g., state manipulation in the local unions' elections, the reorganization of the national unions parallel to the central ministries and agencies (which suggests a better integration between the two), and the setting of a framework by the administration to the discussion preceding and during the CTC national congress. Direct state control over the labor force has been reinforced with a better system

of identification, record-keeping, measurement of output, and worker-absenteeism control.

7. Increasing political pressure to integrate private agriculture into the state sector as is common in Eastern Europe with the exception of Poland. There have not been major structural changes in the association of small farmers (ANAP). This organization, however, is expected to do political work on its members so that they will expand sales to the state *("acopio")*, reduce production for their own consumption, and totally integrate their land into the state sector. Those employed by private farmers are also under pressure to shift their services to the state farms.

8. Reorganization of the main youth organization (UJC) to expand its membership, improve the latter's political education, and cooperate with the administration in a series of measures to correct failures in the work with youth. These measures include reducing the number of school dropouts through drafting by militarily organized labor squads (e.g., UMAP, Centennial Column, EJT); attacking juvenile delinquency by reducing the age of criminal liability and introducing tougher sanctions for certain crimes; and fighting Western fashions, customs, and behavior to avoid differentiation and rebellious attitudes and strengthen unity and compliance among the youth.

9. Politicalization of and tighter control over education and culture. A more rigid line has been introduced in ideological and cultural affairs to impede deviation from official thought, demand more militant works from writers and artists, put a halt to Western influences on art, centralize control over and politicize the communications media, and request unconditional support of the Revolution from Western advisors, magazine writers, jurors in cultural contests, and visitors.

The image projected in the second half of 1970 by Castro's promised reform was of a decentralized, democratic, independent, and mass-participation movement, in the mobilization style that was typical in Cuba during the 1960s. In real life there has been an institutionalization trend characterized by central controls, dogmatism, and administrative-bureaucratic features resembling the Soviet system. What were the causes of the different outcome?

In trying to explain the democratization movement it could be argued that Castro became genuinely convinced of both his mistakes and the truth of his Marxist critics, hence deciding to follow their advice. Most of the critical books and articles were published before Castro's (and other leaders') self-criticism began, and both this and many of the proposed measures had a remarkable similarity to those of the critics. The democratization movement could have also been a desperate effort to mobilize the Cuban masses behind their charismatic leader in order to increase his leverage with the Soviets and maintain independence, at least in internal politics. Some of Castro's proposed measures were certainly unconventional by Soviet standards and had a strong element of mobilization, e.g., city-district organizations—integrated by representatives of mass organizations —to supervise both the administration and the party; and collective bodies—also integrated by delegates from unions as well as mass organizations—to manage state enterprises.

The first point in the above argument has a weakness: If Castro was genuinely convinced that his Marxist critics were correct, why did he end by denouncing them as CIA agents? In an opposite direction it could be argued that the democratization movement was a fake, a temporary device to compensate for Castro's errors, the erosion of his charisma, and the disenchantment that followed the 1970 sugar-crop disaster. Castro may have used the suggestions of his critics for that purpose but he never really intended to change the autocratic nature of the regime. A more sophisticated explanation has been offered by the French Marxist planner, Charles Bettelheim. According to him, if there was an initial commitment to democratization it was rapidly dropped because it generated a chain reaction of criticism that frightened the leadership. The French planner adds that Dumont's and Karol's books were circulating secretly in Cuba and being read by the rebellious youth who were eager to learn the facts and alternative solutions to the island's problems. Thus Castro had to totally discredit the authors by accusing them of being imperialist agents.[114]

If Castro launched the democratization movement either as a desperate, futile attempt to assert Cuba's independence, faked it, or initially tried it seriously but dropped it afterwards, increasing Soviet influence is a steady variable to explain the eventual predominance of centralist-dogmatic institutionalization. In chapter 1, it was explained how the U.S.S.R. has increased its leverage over Cuba and induced Castro to revise the ideology that he so vehemently endorsed during the Sino-Guevarist stage so as to adapt it to conventional Soviet thought. Chapter 2 offered abundant evidence to support the viewpoint that Cuban economic organization in the 1970s has been dramatically transformed to comply with the Soviet system. The modification of Cuban foreign policy, to be discussed in chapter 4, also shows the Soviet imprint. The changes in government and society analyzed in this chapter uphold the hypothesis that the current process of institutionalization has been basically molded in the Soviet die.

4

Foreign Policy:
Multiple Roads to Socialism

Isolated from this hemisphere for most of the 1960s, the Cuban leaders heartily embraced the principle that the guerrilla *foco* was the only road to socialism. An inter-American organization was established in Havana to promote continental revolution. The government launched armed expeditions to, supported subversion in, and trained guerrillas from Latin American countries. They rejected any possibility of reestablishing relations with countries that did not meet their strict criteria of revolution and launched a violent campaign against the United States.

Under the new policy of the 1970s, the pendulum has slowly swung to the other extreme: "non-guerrilla" roads to socialism have been accepted; the exportation of the revolution has been reduced to rhetorical proclamations of support; diplomatic and/or trade relations have been reestablished at one point or another with a dozen Latin American countries, most of which are not revolutionary; discrepancies in relations with several guerrilla leaders and insurrectional movements in Latin America have occurred; and conditions have been set for negotiations with the United States. At the same time, the Organization of American States (OAS) has liberalized its policy to accept diverse socio-politico-economic systems while the United States has ended its involvement in Vietnam and improved relations with China and the U.S.S.R. Paradoxically, in this era of realpolitik, a rapprochement between the United States and Cuba has not yet crystallized, but it is difficult to imagine that the 1970s will end without it.

Realpolitik with Latin America

In January 1962 the OAS agreed to expel Cuba from the OAS, alleging that Cuba's self-proclaimed socialism, Marxism-Leninism, and military links with the Soviet Union were incompatible with the inter-American system. In July 1964 the OAS, responding to evidence presented by Venezuela of a Cuban-armed expedition, agreed to cut diplomatic, economic, and transportation links with Cuba. At the time, only Mexico, Chile, and Uruguay opposed the sanctions, but eventually the last two countries accepted the OAS decision. Cuba resorted to increased aid to revolutionary groups in Latin America as the only way to break its hemispheric isolation. In addition, in 1966–1967, Che Guevara, Regis Debray, and Fidel Castro proclaimed that the rural guerrilla *foco* "a la Cuba" was the only road for revolution in Latin America.

In the late 1960s, three events induced Cuba to stop sending armed expeditions abroad and to dramatically reduce its aid to Latin American guerrillas and revolutionary movements: the death of Che Guevara and the concomitant failure of his guerrillas in Bolivia (as well as previous failures in Argentina, Guatemala, Peru, and Venezuela); the deterioration of the Cuban economy which forced an inward concentration of all the nation's resources and efforts; and the rapprochement with the U.S.S.R., which allowed the latter to exert pressure on Cuba to normalize her relations with Latin America.[1] Early in 1970, Venezuelan guerrilla leader Douglas Bravo accused Castro of abandoning continental revolution for consolidating socialism in his own country, as Stalin had done in the U.S.S.R. in the 1930s. The premier answered defending his nation's "right and duty" to improve its economy and warned that, in the future, guerrilla fighters would have to meet Cuban criteria to receive aid.[2] Since 1970, almost nothing has been heard from the Organization of Latin American Solidarity (OLAS), founded in Havana in 1967 to promote continental revolution. There are occasional reassurances in Castro's sppeches that Cuba is still supporting revolution in Latin America, but these seem to be rhetorical statements except perhaps for the training in Cuba of a selected group of Latin American revolutionaries.

In trying to break its hemispheric isolation and under pressure from the U.S.S.R., Cuba has become increasingly compromising with the socio-economic-political systems of other Latin American countries, first accepting the "progressive military," then "democratic socialism," and finally conventional military regimes and representative democracies. In mid–1969, Castro had set three preconditions in order for Latin American countries to restore relations with Cuba: (a) rejection of the OAS sanctions; (b) condemnation of the "crimes" committed against Cuba by "Yankee imperialism"; and (c) revolution. He then said that Cuba would never return to the OAS and would wait as long as necessary (ten, twenty, thirty years) until all Latin American countries would revolt and establish the Organization of Revolutionary States of Latin America.[3] Less than one year later, Castro replaced all these preconditions with a new one: that the country behave independently of the United States.[4]

Peru was the first country that offered Cuba an opportunity to practice the new realpolitik when, in 1968, General Juan Velasco Alvarado overthrew the democratic, but weak and inefficient, government of Belaunde Terry, proclaimed a revolution, and nationalized the U.S. oil industry. Since then Cuban-Peruvian relations have warmed steadily. In 1969 Castro hailed the Peruvian leaders as a "new phenomenon," that of "a group of progressive military playing a revolutionary role"; in 1970, generous Cuban aid was given to help the victims of the devastating Peruvian earthquake; in the fall of 1971, Velasco invited a Cuban delegation to attend a meeting of the UNCTAD's Group of 77 held in Lima; and in late 1971, Castro made a stopover at the Lima airport (on his way back to Cuba from Chile) and met Velasco. Early in 1972, Peru presented a motion at the OAS requesting that its members be free to individually reestablish relations with Cuba if they wanted. The motion was defeated but, in July, Peru reestablished relations with Cuba.

For a brief period, under the rule of leftist General Torres in 1970–1971, there was a chance that Bolivia would repeat the Peruvian example; but the military coup of conservative General Banzer in late 1971 erased that possibility.

Since 1971, Cuba has been courting Panama's military regime led by General Omar Torrijos. He has introduced a few minor socio-economic reforms and has challenged the United States over the Panama Canal. At the end of 1971, two vessels under Panamanian flag were captured by the Cuban Navy, which alleged that the vessels had previously launched incursions against Cuba and that the captain of one of them (a Cuban by birth and a U.S. citizen) was a CIA agent. The U.S. government offered its aid to Panama and requested from Cuba the return of the vessels and the captain. Castro immediately denounced this as a U.S. plot to divert Panamanian attention from the canal and damage relations with Cuba. He invited Torrijos to send a plane to Havana to pick up all the crewmen who had not participated in acts of aggression. A Panamanian delegation soon arrived, heard the confession of those crewmen accused by Cuba, accepted the conditions, and hailed Castro for respecting Panama's sovereignty.[5] In 1972, Panama supported the Peruvian motion at the OAS and Panamanian Air Force planes made regular trips to Cuba carrying university professors and students as well as politicians. Later in the year, Torrijos followed the Cuban precedent at Guantánamo Base by refusing to collect the U.S. annual rent for the Canal Zone. In 1973 the conflict over the canal was taken by Panama to the UN Security Council with strong support from Cuba, Peru, the U.S.S.R., and China, and against U.S. objections. During council meetings held in March in Panama City, General Torrijos condemned the embargo of Cuba and Foreign Minister Juan Antonio Tack announced that Panama would soon recognize Cuba.[6] One year later, however, a settlement between Panama and the United States over the canal issue seemed imminent and Panama had not yet formally reestablished relations with Cuba.

In 1969, the Chilean Christian Democratic government of Eduardo Frei initiated trade exchanges with Cuba and in June, 1970 signed a two-year trade agreement for $11 million. Later in the year, the Marxist candidate of the Popular Front (*Unidad Popular,* composed of Socialists, Communists, Radicals, and a leftist split of the Christian Democrats—MAPU), and Castro's friend, Salvador Allende, was elected president. Ten days after taking office, Allende reestablished diplomatic relations with Cuba, and early in 1971, a new trade agreement (increasing the trade volume by $6 million) was signed by both countries.[7] Castro and Allende exchanged visits in 1971 and 1972. Nevertheless, relations between the two nations were broken in September of 1973 by the Chilean military government immediately after the coup was implemented.

In 1971, Castro supported Uruguay's Popular Front (Frente Amplio) in that nation's elections. This front, more mixed a coalition than that of Chile, was composed of splits from the two traditional parties ("Blanco" and "Colorado") together with Communists, Socialists, and Christian Democrats and was led by retired General Liber Seregni. An illegal movement of urban guerrillas, the Tupamaros, could not participate in the elections and, although manifesting doubts that it could solve the problem, did not oppose the Frente. The latter lost the election to the conservative candidate of the incumbent party, Juan M. Bordaberry. In 1972–1973 the military crushed the Tupamaros, closed down the congress, banned the Communist party, and shut the door to any potential resumption of relations with Cuba.

A surprising rapprochement took place in 1971–1972 between Cuba and the conventional government of Ecuador led by the seventy-eight-year-old politician and quasi-dictator, Velasco Ibarra. He had not introduced a single revolutionary measure in his term (nor in his previous two brief periods as president) but seized some fifty U.S. fishing ships that had entered the unilaterally established 200-mile territorial waters of Ecuador. (The country is strategically important to Cuba because it is expected to become the second largest Latin American oil exporter by 1975.) In the Soviet-Cuban communiqué released on the occasion of Premier Kosygin's visit to Havana, both parties hailed Ecuador's "independent posture" (as well as that of Panama). On his way back from Chile, Castro made a stop at Quito's airport and met Velasco Ibarra and part of his cabinet. The warming relationship was interrupted in early 1972 by a military coup that overthrew Velasco Ibarra (for the third time in his career!). The new military regime has been cautious in its statements and, although siding in 1972 with the Peruvians at the OAS meeting, did not follow them in immediately reestablishing relations with Cuba. In March 1973, during the ECLA (Economic Commission for Latin America) meetings held in Quito, the chief of the Cuban delegation, Rodríguez, met with Ecuadorian president General Guillermo Rodríguez Lara. When asked by journalists if the reestablishment of relations between the two countries was imminent, Rodríguez diplomatically replied "we are not in a hurry."[8]

Mexico never accepted the OAS decision to isolate Cuba. Diplomatic relations and small trade continued uninterrupted although several conflicts created tension and coolness between the two countries. Early in 1972, the situation apparently changed when, for the first time since Cuba's revolutionary takeover, an exchange of foreign trade missions took place. Cuba is interested in buying Mexican lubricants, manufactured products, and medicines (the latter suggests that the expected Soviet aid to develop a pharmaceutical industry in Cuba has not materialized) and receiving technical experience in the industrial processing of minerals and petroleum derivatives, in exchange for tobacco, rum, and minerals. Mexico's Foreign Trade Bank offered to finance the operation and an agreement was signed in March 1973. Two months later Mexico and Cuba signed an agreement on the treatment of hijackers.[9]

Jamaica and Trinidad and Tobago entered the OAS in the late 1960s. Instead of alleging that they were not bound by the 1964 OAS decision, the two countries abstained from establishing diplomatic and trade relations with Cuba. The two nations have rather conventional regimes, democratically elected, and at one point, Trinidad and Tobago accused Cuba of training some of its citizens in revolutionary warfare. The situation changed in 1971–1972, however. An exchange of trade missions took place between Cuba and Trinidad and Tobago in late 1971, and a more liberal party gained power in Jamaica early in 1972. Both countries voted in favor of the Peruvian motion in the OAS in the spring of 1972, and Castro hailed them for doing so. In a conference of Commonwealth Caribbean leaders held in Port-of-Spain in October, Jamaica and Trinidad and

Tobago (as well as Barbados and Guyana, the first of which entered the OAS in the early 1970s) decided to establish diplomatic relations with Cuba and the decision was implemented in December, 1972. Castro paid short visits to Guyana and Trinidad-Tobago in September 1973 and met, in Port-of-Spain, the prime ministers of the four English-speaking Caribbean nations and thanked them for reestablishing relations with Cuba.[10]

The unexpected occurred in Argentina when in rapid succession President-General Alejandro Lanusse convoked presidential elections. These were freely held in March 1973 and won by the Peronist candidate, Dr. Héctor Cámpora, who was inaugurated as president in May. Cuban president Dorticós was invited to the inauguration and three days later Argentina and Cuba reestablished diplomatic relations. New elections, followed by the victory of General Juan Perón, consolidated the rapprochement between the two nations. In August, Argentina granted Cuba a credit of $1.2 billion to purchase agricultural, road-building, and railroad equipment. The Argentine Minister of Economy, José Gelbard, announced later that branches of U.S. corporations in his country would have to cooperate in view of the new Argentine trade policies with Cuba. At the end of the year, Chrysler-Fevre began negotiations with the Cuban trade mission in Buenos Aires, and General Motors-Argentina offered to sell 1,500 vehicles to the island. Ford rapidly joined the group. The three automobile corporations then requested the necessary authorization from the U.S. Treasury in order to sell vehicles to Cuba. In early 1974, Minister Gelbard headed a trade delegation to Havana which included representatives of the three U.S. corporations, and declared that the latter would sell to Cuba regardless of the U.S. Treasury's decision. The authorization was finally granted by Washington in April.[11]

In Central America surprising changes began to take place. At the end of 1972, Cuba sent two "medical brigades" to help the victims of the earthquake that destroyed Managua (interestingly, the same gesture that opened the door to the Peruvians), and they were received by the Minister of Public Health.[12] Cuba stated that this was an act of solidarity to the suffering people of Nicaragua and did not necessarily mean support of Nicaraguan dictator Anastasio Somoza, Jr. But even this gesture would have been difficult to imagine three years before. On the other hand, then Costa Rican president José Figueres (another former archenemy of Castro), addressing a meeting of Cuban exiles in Puerto Rico in 1973, advised them to be realistic (in view of the U.S. rapprochement with China) and to be open-minded of the possibility of rapprochement between Cuba and the United States.[13] In late 1973, Honduras renewed trade relations with Cuba signing a $2.3 million agreement to buy sugar from the island.[14]

Finally, relations with Venezuela, the nation which in 1963 had requested the OAS to impose sanctions against Cuba, improved considerably since 1969 as a result of a change in attitude by the Christian Democrat government. The first step was taken by President Rafael Caldera's "pacification program" which included legalization of the Venezuelan Communist party, amnesty to revolutionary activists who agreed to respect the democratic process, and relaxation of tensions with Cuba. In 1972 top Venezuelan officials from the Ministries of Education and Agriculture visited Cuba; there were professional, scholastic, and sports exchanges; the Cuban press agency *Prensa Latina* was allowed to establish a branch in Caracas; and one of the two Cuban guerrillas arrested in the 1963 landing was freed. (Another Cuban guerrilla captured in 1967 was freed in early 1974.) Early in 1973 Caldera stated that the guerrillas in Venezuela had disappeared, that Cuba's conflicts with other Latin American countries had been considerably reduced, that the normalization process between Venezuela and Cuba was evolving positively, that his government was endorsing Cuba's entrance into international agencies (e.g., the Group of 77), and that although Venezuela would not formally present the Cuban case in the next OAS General Assembly, the theme would be discussed informally. The assembly held in April was headed by Venezuelan foreign minister Arístides Calvani who played a crucial role in obtaining approval for the new doctrine of "ideological pluralism"—which meant the acceptance by the OAS of nations with divergent socio-politico-economic systems, including Marxist ones.[15] At the same time the OAS assembly was taking place, the Christian Democrat presidential candidate Lorenzo Fernández was in Moscow discussing with Soviet leaders the possibility of shipping oil from Venezuela to Cuba.[16] In his 1973 May Day speech, Castro for the first time openly courted Venezuela by welcoming its recent step to annul the commercial treaty with the United States and announcing that Cuba would support the Venezuelan government "regardless of its economic system" in case of a serious conflict with international oil corporations.[17] In June an OAS commission approved a Venezuelan motion by which a majority of votes (and not two-thirds as before) is now enough to lift the sanctions against Cuba. Less than one month later an anti-hijacking agreement was signed between Venezuela and Cuba. In September Castro praised as "progressive" the Venezuelan action in the OAS and said that Cuba would welcome a visit of President Caldera to Havana. The following month a Venezuelan official delegation led by a minister and close friend of Caldera went to Cuba spurring the rumor that relations would be reestablished immediately.[18] This warming trend was temporarily halted in December 1973 when the opposition's candidate, Carlos Andrés Pérez (from Acción Democrática), was chosen as president in national elections. In his platform Pérez had sustained a more conservative policy vis-a-vis Cuba but, after his inauguration in March 1974, there were indications that he would continue Caldera's policy.

The previous pages show that, in spite of several setbacks, Cuba has assumed an increasingly compromising attitude vis-a-vis Latin American countries[19] with divergent revolutionary stands; the Chilean Marxist government of Allende; a group of nations that have proclaimed themselves revolutionaries but are mostly reformist (e.g., Mexico, Panama and Peru), or have not changed their status quo at all (as in Argentina and Ecuador); and a group of conventional regimes that do not pretend to be revolutionary (e.g., Barbados, Guyana, Jamaica, Trinidad and Tobago, and Venezuela). A Hungarian journalist posed the problem to Castro while he was in Chile, asking him: "You have said a number of times in your speeches that there are many ways to achieve socialism; could you give us a general picture of the Latin American scene in this respect?" Castro answered employing the "Cantinflas style" (the deliberately confusing and contradictory manner which the famous Mexican comedian, Mario Moreno, uses to get away from difficult situations):

> I don't think I ever said that there were many ways, I might have said that there was more than one way, which remains to be proven and, to a certain extent, is being proved. Also, that new variants might come up. . . . Here's a new way: the Chilean process. A variant which may very well set the beginning of a process whose future we cannot predict, as in the case of Peru.

A Chilean journalist tried to get a more concrete definition from the Cuban premier by asking: "In view of the experience of the last ten years of revolutionary struggle in Latin America, do you think that the theory of the revolutionary nucleus [the guerrilla *foco*] is now subordinate to other forms of struggle or is that theoretical stand still valid?" Castro diplomatically chose to remain silent.[20]

Conflicts with Old Allies and Friends

The new realpolitik of the Cuban Revolution has generated a series of conflicts due to the abandonment of Castroite revolutionaries who oppose in their countries the governments with whom Cuba has reached a détente. There are also contradictions between Cuba's manifested principles or ideology and those of the new allies. As Karol has pointed out, in 1968 Castro's criterion for sorting friend from foe was their prevailing attitude toward the U.S.S.R. Three years later, having come to terms with the Soviets, Castro's criterion changed to weigh on his allies' prevailing attitude toward the United States. In both cases, the Cuban leader was willing to accept as an ally a country which shared his antagonism toward his main enemy at that time, neglecting the internal system of such an ally. This inconsistency was masterfully presented to Castro while in Chile by a journalist from Iceland:

> You have self-determined yourself as a revolutionary but at

the same time you said that you wanted to have relations with any country that had an independent policy [from the United States]. It seems to me that there is a contradiction between the two positions. One would be nationalistic and the other would be revolutionary. If tomorrow you discover that Ecuador or Argentina offers you good relations [and you decide to accept], you can fall in the same contradictions as the Soviet Union has with its aid to Iran and Bolivia, or as Communist China has with its aid to Pakistan.

Castro answered:

> If you want to be an accurate observer of reality and not a theoretician passing judgment on the problems of this world from an ivory tower . . . you have to understand politics as a principle, one bound by conditions or reality. . . . The thing that would be most displeasing to U.S. imperialism today would be if—in defiance of the accords that imperialism imposed through its colonial administration, which is what the OAS is—various governments should establish relations with Cuba. . . . There would be no contradiction if the government of Ecuador wants to establish diplomatic relations with Cuba. Because we subordinate whatever other differences or whatever other problem exists to the fundamental one: defiance of the dictates of the United States.[21]

The question that could have been asked then was: What about the revolutionaries in Ecuador and the contradictions between that system and Cuba's? This conflict is not a theoretical one but has actually occurred in Peru, Chile, Mexico, Argentina, and other countries. (It could have happened in Bolivia if the 1971 coup had not impeded the rapprochement between Cuba and the military regime led by a man who belonged to the same armed forces which killed Guevara in 1967.)

In 1969, Castro began praising the Peruvian military junta which had kept imprisoned two guerrilla fighters who had been pro-Castroites: Hugo Blanco (condemned to twenty-five years) and

Héctor Béjar. Both were released at the end of 1970 and took different positions, one against the junta and the other working within it, but both critical of Castro. Blanco's militant antagonism earned him political exile in September 1971; he did not, however, go to Cuba but went to Mexico instead. (His destination could have been the decision of either Blanco or the Cuban government.) He later moved in succession to Argentina, Chile, and back to Mexico. Blanco has stated that when he was leading his guerrillas he did not receive the human and material aid that Cuba claimed it had sent but only the support of Radio Havana. Now "Castro, the guerrilla par excellence, believes it possible that in Peru socialism will come about without destroying the present government by force of arms." Blanco added that he is "disheartened" when he listens to the Cuban radio supporting the military government, "which represents the exploiters" instead of the true revolution.[22] Béjar explained almost at the same time the opposition between the Peruvian and Cuban approaches to continuity and change. He said that he supported the military government of his country because it had assumed a pragmatic and flexible position vis-a-vis sources of financing for development and degree of state control. Thus Peru accepted economic aid from the United States, Japan, the U.S.S.R., and international agencies in order to guarantee the country's independence, as well as domestic private financing to avoid grave economic sacrifices to its people and to facilitate increasing political freedom in the nation. Conversely, Béjar suggested, Cuba had substituted dependence on the Soviets for its former dependence on the United States and had collectivized everything, subjecting its people to tremendous hardships and establishing absolute state control in politics.[23]

In Chile, the conflict between the MIR (a Castroite type of movement) and Allende's Front put Castro in a difficult position. The MIR encouraged the illegal occupation of land, thus disobeying Allende's warnings; it also wanted either abolition or radical reform of the democratic institutions that Allende had promised to preserve; finally, the MIR (together with some socialists) demanded faster and deeper revolutionary change, while Allende tried to consolidate the process itself. This conflict came to the fore in the last days of

Castro's visit to Chile. Upon his arrival at Santiago airport, Castro cautiously said: "We aren't holding our Revolution up as a model. . . . We don't claim that we are free of defects, that we haven't made any mistakes. . . . It would be ridiculous for us to tell you: 'Do as we have done.' "[24] In his farewell speech, he stated, certainly pleasing Allende: "We didn't come to teach [but] to learn, to see something extraordinary . . . taking place in Chile. Something more than unique: unusual! It is a revolutionary process [he had pointed out before that "a revolutionary process is not a revolution"] practically the first in humanity's history . . . in which revolutionaries are trying to carry out changes peacefully." But then (taking the MIR's stand), he bluntly rejected that he had gone to Chile to learn about elections, parliament, and freedom of the press and suggested that these were "anachronisms" which would eventually be eradicated by the people. According to him, these institutions were used to confuse, deceive, and divide the peasants, the workers, and the middle class, trying to win them over to the "counter-revolutionary cause," thus weaking the revolutionary forces. "In this ideological struggle, the odds are against the revolutionaries; [because they] are not equal to the reactionaries." Castro then explained the sophisticated techniques that the opposition used in Chile (and that had bothered him, such as indiscreet questions posed by journalists and criticism from students) and claimed that the revolutionaries had shown little ability in mobilizing the masses (which also upset him when his farewell speech in Santiago's stadium had a poor attendance). Cuba, Castro assured, had a greater power for mobilization than Chile because the former had mechanisms and instruments for mobilization that the latter lacked. Castro concluded by saying that what he had learned in Chile made him identify more with the Cuban model.[25] Thus, in the last minute, he broke his promise to avoid interference in Chilean affairs, advising Allende to get rid of all those institutions that made possible the "unique" Chilean revolutionary process and to adopt instead the state mobilization techniques.

The military coup of September 11, 1973, broke a forty-year tradition of constitutionalism in Chile, overthrew a democratically elected government, and took Allende's life. It was also a dramatic blow to the attempt of reaching socialism through democratic, peaceful means and, in some way, a confirmation of the Castroite position. Concerning the latter, it could be conversely argued that Allende's position was the only one possible and that the radicalization of the revolution would have only precipitated the military intervention. Castro strongly condemned the coup, blamed the U.S. government as its instigator and organizer, declared that Allende had won a place of honor among the great martyrs, invited Mrs. Allende and her daughter to visit Cuba, and launched a campaign against the military junta. And yet, when asked if Cuba would try to reestablish socialism in Chile by exporting the revolution to that nation, Castro rejected that action as impossible. Even more significant was the moderation with which Cuban officials and the press handled the Christian Democrat support of the coup, presenting it as a decision of personalities and rightist factions of the party but not of the movement as a whole.[26] This cautious attitude was probably intended to avoid further embarrassment and loss of support to the Venezuelan Christian Democrats with whom Cuba was reaching an understanding at the time.

The Cuban leadership paid a high price for trying to save its link with Mexico, the only Latin American country with which the island had diplomatic relations, airline connections, and some trade in the second half of the 1960s. Friction between the two countries was common. Mexico derived an immediate gain from the Cuban-U.S. split: an enlarged U.S. sugar quota. The Mexicans steadily improved their relations with the Americans as the presidential meetings of Díaz Ordaz/Johnson and Echeverría/Nixon exemplified, and the Mexican police collaborated with U.S. intelligence in checking travelers to Cuba (stamping their passports and taking photos of them). Cuban trade with Mexico was small and systematically at a deficit. In 1969 a few Mexican airplanes were hijacked to Cuba, and a member of the Mexican Embassy in Havana was accused of being a CIA agent by Castro and was expelled from the country.[27] In 1968, hundreds of Mexican students who were protesting against the government in the Plaza de Tlatelolco were killed, wounded, or imprisoned; several university professors and intellectual figures were also sent to jail. Press reports were published suggesting that Cuba was behind the student revolt, an alleged leftist plot to disrupt the Olympic games to be held in Mexico City. To the dismay of the Mexican left, Cuba did not condemn the massacre and massive imprisonment and did send its athletes to the Olympics. In 1971, the Mexican government captured a small guerrilla *foco* and reported that its members had been trained in North Korea with the U.S.S.R. serving as an intermediary. In the news media campaign that followed, some newspapers suggested that Cuba was also involved in the affair. But the Cubans again remained silent, probably because they did not want to jeopardize the exchange of trade missions that took place a few months later.

The establishment of relations between Cuba and Guyana was a serious blow to the opposition, the People's Progressive Party of Cheddi Jagan, a close friend of Castro in the 1960s. Almost at the same time that relations were established, a pro-government Guyanan magazine reported that the friendship between Castro and Jagan had been dissolved because of the embezzlement of $20 million sent previously to Jagan from Castro.[28] In his visit to Guyana in September 1973, Castro was asked about Cuba's position on reactionary regimes and the kind of struggle that should be fought against them. He answered: "It's for the people and not for us to decide which form of struggle is necessary."[29]

Most revealing was Cuba's cautious attitude vis-a-vis the ill-fated expedition of Colonel Francisco Caamaño Deñó to the Dominican Republic in February 1973. Caamaño was the leader of the 1965 Dominican uprising crushed by the U.S. intervention; since 1967 he had disappeared, although it was generally assumed that he was in Cuba. He landed in the Dominican Republic with a tiny guerrilla group and a week later had been killed and his guerrillas disbanded. The Cuban press reported the tragic events factually by using international news-agencies' wires (e.g., UPI, AFP, EFE) and did not endorse the action. One surviving guerrilla and a nephew of Caamaño, who escaped to Mexico, reported that the expedition was not launched from Cuba but from the island of Guadeloupe in the Caribbean.[30]

Changes within the OAS

Cuba's compromising attitude regarding the Latin American countries that "behave independently from the U.S.A." has been paralleled with consistent verbal attacks against other military regimes (Argentina until May 1973, Bolivia after September 1971, Chile since 1973, Brazil and Paraguay the entire time), representative democracies (Colombia, Costa Rica, and, until 1970, Venezuela) and twilight-zone systems (the Dominican Republic, El Salvador, Guatemala, Honduras, and Uruguay). All are indiscriminantly despised as "imperialist puppets" or "Yankee lackeys." Training of selective revolutionaries from some of these countries apparently continues; and Cuba, at least rhetorically, also claims to be actively supporting revolutionary forces within those same countries. These countries (together with the United States) have strongly opposed a revision of the 1962–1964 OAS agreements. In general, the less legitimate these countries' governtmental bases and the more they are maintained by repression, the stronger their opposition to Cuba. (Many of these countries, in fact, have exaggerated the Castroite threat to get more economic and military aid from the United States.) The most democratic regimes have been more flexible in this matter in spite of real physical attacks originated by Cuba.

For a decade Castro systematically rejected the possibility of Cuba's return to the OAS, abhorring it as a "putrid, revolting den of corruption," a "disgusting, discredited cesspool" and a "ministry of colonies of the United States." At one point Castro said that Cuba would return to the OAS only if the "imperialists and their puppets were kicked out first"; more recently he spoke of the substitution of the OAS first by the Organization of Revolutionary States of Latin America and later by the Union of Peoples of Latin America. (It should be noted that the second title, suggested in 1971, conveniently excluded the word "Revolutionary.")[31]

The position of OAS officials in the matter has been an embarrassing one: violently rejected by Castro, strongly criticized by several Latin American countries, and confronting strong opposition to change from the most authoritarian-conservative countries in the area in an awkward marriage with the powerful United States. In

November 1971, trying to avoid a repetition of the Chilean example (Allende individually reestablished relations with Cuba), the Secretary General of the OAS, Galo Plaza, began consultations in Mexico on the "normalization" of relations with Cuba. Besides the support of the openly favorable countries, he apparently received an endorsement from both Bolivia (then under leftist Torres) and the open-minded democratic countries. But the strong opposition of conservative military regimes and that of the United States put an end to the move.[32]

In the spring of 1971, Nixon's overtures to China raised the possibility that Cuba would be next. The majority of the OAS members became fearful of losing their scapegoat and bait for juicy U.S. aid as Taiwan had done. The open-minded minority showed concern over an embarrassing Cuban-U.S. agreement behind their backs. Galo Plaza hurried to ask the White House and the State Department to keep him, and the OAS members, informed of any changes in policy toward Cuba and resumed his efforts to find a satisfactory compromise within the OAS framework. The Cuban Ministry of Foreign Relations quickly rejected any move to restore Cuba to OAS membership but welcomed the restoration of relations with Latin American countries on an individual basis. Toward the end of the year, Peru presented a motion at the OAS freeing its members to make individual decisions on the matter but later withdrew the motion. In May 1972, Peru reintroduced the motion which was defended at an extraordinary meeting of the OAS by Chancellor General Mercado Jorrín.[33] The final vote (thirteen against, seven in favor, and three abstentions) showed some surprises: Colombia and Costa Rica (reportedly favorable) voted no, and Argentina and Venezuela (the first reportedly against, the second in favor) abstained.[34] Castro's strong statement from Sofia, at the same time that the meeting was taking place, rejecting any "neutralization" of Cuba and endorsing the Latin American revolution (see below) could have affected the voting adversely.

The changes that occurred in Latin America in the second half of 1972 and the first half of 1973 significantly altered the OAS voting pattern in the Cuban case. In April 1973 the majority of the OAS members accepted the new doctrine of "ideological pluralism" and

Galo Plaza stated that possibly the next General Assembly would lift the sanctions placed in 1964 against Cuba.[35] At the time, there were in the OAS eleven countries solidly in favor of lifting the sanctions, six strongly against, and seven weren't clearly decided. This was a remarkable shift in one year, but still only eight votes (one-third of the membership) were needed to maintain the sanctions. On May Day 1973, Castro said that the new doctrine of "ideological pluralism" made the 1962 OAS resolution (declaring the Cuban Marxist system incompatible with the "inter-American system") null and void. And yet he did not help break the deadlock by stating that it was the OAS that was incompatible with Marxism-Leninism and by rejecting a return to the OAS unless the United States was excluded from the organization. (He also added a new condition: that the OAS headquarters be moved to a Latin American country.)[36]

In June 1973 an OAS commission approved the Venezuelan motion substituting a simple majority of twelve votes instead of the previously required two-thirds majority of fifteen votes to lift the sanctions against Cuba and allowing each country to individually decide about diplomatic and trade relations. Two countries previously reported as not clearly decided (Colombia and Costa Rica) voted in favor of the amendment raising to thirteen the number of those favorable to rapprochement. The military coup in Chile dramatically turned a militant positive vote into an equally vehement negative one. Still the necessary twelve votes seemed assured at the time, but the change of government in Venezuela raised some doubt, at least temporarily, on the future policy of this country and the majority vanished. Furthermore, these changes induced a freeze in the attitude of most undecided countries which will move in favor of a rapprochement only after a decision is reached by a majority within the OAS. Finally, in early 1974 the United States took two significant steps to ease tensions in Latin America: it reached an agreement over expropriation of U.S. property with Peru and established a basis for negotiation over the canal issue with Panama. The results of these events were clear in the Inter-American Conference of Chancellors held in Mexico City in February. Although the issue of U.S. economic sanctions had been included in the agenda and five Latin

American countries had informally requested a discussion of relations
with Cuba, the conference did not reach any conclusion on the
subject. However, in another hemisphere foreign ministers' meeting
held in Washington in April 1974, Argentina proposed (supported by
Mexico, Peru, and Venezuela) that Cuba be invited to the next of
such meetings to be held in Buenos Aires in March 1975. The
proposal was adopted almost unanimously. The United States did not
object but asked Argentina to consult all the countries involved to
see whether there was a "consensus" to extend the invitation to
Cuba. Mexico's foreign minister Emilio Rabasa reported that, after
conferring at the beginning of April in Havana with Castro, he was
convinced Cuba would send a representative to a "constructive"
hemispheric meeting even if Cuba was unwilling to rejoin the OAS
formally.[37] (For changes in the voting pattern of OAS members on
the Cuban issue, see table 6.)

TABLE 6

OAS Members' Stand on the Cuban Issue: 1970-1974[a]

Stand	1970	1972	1973	1974
In favor of rapprochement	4	7	13	10
With diplomatic relations	1	3	8	7
Without diplomatic relations	3	4	5	3
Dubious	5	3	5	6
Against	14	13	6	8
Total	23	23	24	24

[a]Mid-year

Sources: See explanation in the text.

In early 1974 the United States had been left siding, on the Cuban
issue, with the most authoritarian-conservative regimes of the
hemisphere (e.g., Bolivia, Brazil, Chile, Haiti, Paraguay) which
violently reject any change in the status quo. Is a rapprochement
between Havana and Washington possible?

The Conditions for a U.S.-Cuban Rapprochement

In the late 1960s, a U.S.-Cuban rapprochement was mainly the subject of intellectual discussion with a few practical overtures which did not produce the expected results.[38] In the 1970s, however, an era of realpolitik has begun which has created better opportunities for negotiation: on the U.S. side, the understanding with China, agreements with the U.S.S.R., and the peace settlement in Vietnam; on the Cuban side, the decline in the exportation of the revolution to Latin America and a more compromising attitude toward divergent systems in the area. Until now, however, there have been only minor changes in the positions of the chief leaders of the two countries, and the conditions for negotiation established by both seem irreconcilable.[39]

In October 1969—with an eye on the increasing number of military and authoritarian regimes in Latin America—President Nixon pragmatically stated that, in the future, the United States would deal with these countries realistically as they are. This justified the close U.S. economic and military cooperation with Brazil and its compromising policy vis-a-vis Peru. U.S. officials have not mentioned again the incompatibility of the Cuban regime with the inter-American system as a deterrent for normalizing relations between the two countries. (The "inter-American system" was never clearly defined but loosely meant representative democracy plus market economy, a formula which is now absent in most of Latin America and has been substituted within the OAS by the new doctrine of "ideological pluralism.") The U.S. government, however, has not modified its stand in regard to the two other preconditions established for the restoration of relations with Cuba: (1) cutting its military ties with the U.S.S.R., and (2) stopping its subversion in Latin America. Throughout 1970–1973, the president of the United States, the Secretary of State, and the assistant secretaries for Inter-American Affairs reiterated (in reports to the U.S. Congress, the OAS, the Latin American countries, and the news media) that Cuba had not changed its position on these two points.[40] In 1971, the State Department accepted that "Cuba's active assistance to subversive elements was apparently at reduced levels" but pointed to her intransigent rejection of a return to the OAS as proof that the situation was not ripe for a revision.

This deadlock has been slightly altered by events which have aggravated the existing tension: the hijacking of U.S. planes to Cuba; the capture, in early 1970, of a Cuban fishing boat and its crew by a group of Cuban exiles (there were also attacks on Cuban fishing boats in the fall of 1972 and in early and late 1973); the establishment, late in 1970, of a Soviet servicing facility for submarines in the Cuban port of Cienfuegos; the detention and expulsion from the United States, in 1971, of a Cuban delegation that attempted to participate in an international sugar conference held in New Orleans; and the seizure, at the end of that year, of two vessels under Panamanian flag by the Cuban Navy. The latter was probably the gravest incident of all: the State Department qualified it as "an intolerable threat" to free trade and navigation in the Caribbean; Pentagon sources indicated that air and naval units were being placed on alert and that they would go to the aid of any attacked ship under a foreign registry, if the corresponding government requested it; and the navy reported that warships stationed in Guantánamo (that is, in Cuban territory) would be sent to the Caribbean to engage in a potential confrontation with Cuban war vessels.[41]

Only in a few cases have there been positive exchanges between the two nations: in 1971, the entrance of a U.S. volleyball team into Cuba and of a Cuban baseball team into Puerto Rico; in 1972, the attendance of an official U.S. scientific delegation (from the Commerce Department) at an international oceanographic conference held in Havana;[42] and in 1973, the anti-hijacking agreement. The latter had been considered on several occasions and was precipitated when in November 1972 a hijacked airplane almost caused a disaster in both the United States and Cuba. (The hijackers threatened to crash the plane into the Oak Ridge Atomic Center and the landing in Havana presented serious problems because the airplane had been damaged by FBI agents' bullets.) Discussions began immediately through the Swiss Embassy in Havana and the agreement was simultaneously signed in that capital city and Washington on February 15, 1973. The document grants to each nation the right to deport the hijacker of an aircraft or vessel or to try him in its own territory and according to its own law. In the latter case hijacking for "strict political reasons" may be considered as a mitigating or extenuating circumstance providing that the hijacker: (a) was in "real and imminent danger of death"; (b) did not have "a viable alternative for leaving the country"; (c) did not use financial extortion (any funds obtained through this means are to be returned without delay); and (d) did not cause physical injury to members of the crew, passengers, or other persons. These conditions, at least in theory, considerably reduce the probability of political hijacking. Another important clause in the agreement stipulates penalties for those who conspire, prepare, or take part in an expedition to carry out acts of violence against the territory, aircraft, or vessels of the other party.[43] This was obviously intended to protect Cuba against attacks from exiles and may explain why the agreement has received no publicity in the United States.

In the few cases in which the United States and Cuba have had positive exchanges (including the hijacking agreement), top officials from one country or the other rapidly dismissed any hope that the exchange could imply a modification of their respective basic policy.

The United States expects Cuba to break the ice, as former president Nixon indicated in his speech of April 1971 on the U.S.-China understanding: "If the Cuban policy toward us should change, then we would consider changing ours. That is, we would take a step forward. . . . Havana hasn't taken any steps, so relations with Cuba remain frozen." Premier Castro answered saying that there would not be an overture from Cuba and that his country would neither be neutralized nor stop its support of all revolutionary movements in Latin America.[44]

In 1971–1972, Castro spoke several times on his own preconditions for a rapprochement with the United States. When visiting Chile, he remarked that to reach an understanding it would not be necessary for a revolutionary or socialist government to be in office in the United States but just a realistic government ("a president of wide vision and broad understanding") aware of the U.S., Latin American, and world situation and aspirations and, hence, assuming a policy of peace. According to Castro, Nixon, although a realistic man, did not represent those trends and had been aggressive and reactionary in the past: "Nixon will never visit Havana!" Cuba would wait until the proper man is installed in the White House. Two conditions would also have to be met by the ideal government for a normalization of relations with Cuba: (1) an end to the war in Vietnam, and (2) an end to the U.S. role of gendarme in Latin America, that is, its abstaining from any intervention as in the past.[45]

In a press conference in Sofia, Bulgaria, in May 1972, Castro dismissed as false a newspaper report stating that he was planning to meet Nixon in Warsaw: "We are not at all interested in such a meeting [and] would refuse [it]." He then stated that Cuba would never yield to the two U.S. conditions: "We will not give in one iota in this respect." Since Cuba had been able to overcome the most difficult tests posed by the United States, Castro argued that "it would be absolutely senseless for us to make any concessions to the U.S.A. [now]." Then he assumed the same attitude that former president Nixon had taken a year before: "Nixon is the one who's got to do something." He would have to meet, "with no strings attached," the two conditions set by Castro in Chile: (1) an end to the Vietnam war, and (2) an end to U.S. intervention in Latin America; plus two additional ones: (3) lifting the economic embargo of Cuba, and (4) getting the naval base out of Guantánamo. Castro said that Cuba would wait two, four, ten years until such conditions were met and further stated that "Kissinger and all those advisers and 'big brains' will never come to Havana or hold any kind of meeting with us."[46]

In his speech of July 26, 1972, Castro reiterated that Cuba's doors would be closed to "Nixon's cheap politicking and dirty deals." At the same time, he expressed satisfaction at seeing "the advances and new formulations in the policies of the U.S." made at the Democratic Convention and that "one of the presidential candidates [McGovern] was in favor of lifting the blockade against Cuba." However, he violently attacked another point of the Democratic platform which stated that Cuba could not become a Soviet military base. "In our territory we do as we damn please!" And no [U.S.] party platform has any right to establish prerequisites of any kind with regard to Cuba."

Finally he reiterated the four conditions, enumerated in Bulgaria, necessary to begin negotiating the restoration of relations with the United States.[47]

What are the actual possibilities of the U.S. meeting the Cuban conditions or vice versa? It is clear that the socialist system of Cuba is no longer at issue and that the United States has concentrated all its emphasis on external matters. As shown in chapter 1, Cuba's military and economic links with the U.S.S.R. have increased in the last decade, especially in the 1970s; hence, the U.S. demand that Cuba close the door to its Soviet friends has induced the opposite result. Without having some guarantees from the United States first, Cuba could not cut its links with the U.S.S.R. To do so would have left Cuba vulnerable to the United States. The Soviet-Cuban military relationship presented a serious threat to the internal security of the United States in October 1962, but during the Missile Crisis the leaders of the two superpowers reached an agreement. This apparently has been honored by the U.S.S.R., which gave explanations to the United States at the time of the installation of its submarine base in Cienfuegos. (In early 1974, Dr. Kissinger apparently accepted these realities and indicated that the United States was not holding this condition as before—see below.) The second U.S. condition was directed mainly at protecting the security of the American allies in Latin America. In many cases, however, those allies exaggerated the real threat in order to increase U.S. aid; in others, they managed (with or without U.S. aid) to capture the expeditions or defeat the guerrillas coming from Cuba. Since 1968, the island has turned inward, dramatically reducing its efforts to export the revolution. With its increasingly compromising attitude toward divergent systems in Latin America—as shown in this study—Cuba has proven that she can be a peaceful neighbor. (The Soviet interest in normalizing the Cuban situation in the Western Hemisphere has been an important factor in this change;[48] thus, the increasing Soviet leverage on Cuba has paradoxically helped in closing the gap to meet one of the two U.S. conditions for negotiation while widening the gap in the other.) And yet the Cuban leaders could not afford to publicly admit that they were another paper tiger and thus have continued their mostly rhetorical support of the revolutionary movements in the area. If the United States would drop its two conditions (this action preferably taking place within the OAS, perhaps with the United States supporting a motion similar to that presented by Peru in 1972) and if a rapprochement were eventually to take place, the two U.S. security objectives would probably be achieved anyway: peaceful relations with the United States and Latin America could result in the increased independence of Cuba vis-a-vis the U.S.S.R. and in an even more conventional foreign policy of the island toward its neighbors.

The first condition set by the Cubans has been met already with the end of the war in Vietnam. (In his speeches of December 1972 and May 1973 Castro dropped this condition.) Concerning the second condition, the last open U.S. intervention in Latin America occurred more than nine years ago in the Dominican Republic; in view of the U.S. experience there and in Vietnam, it is doubtful that such an action would be repeated. Certainly the United States could promise to abstain from intervention provided that the Cubans do the same. The third condition set by the Cubans (raised to the first condition on May 1 by Castro, who added that it should precede any discussion and be unconditional) could be accepted without any significant disadvantages to the United States and probably with some gain. The economic embargo caused serious problems to Cuba at the time of its inception, but most of them have since been overcome. Still some difficulties remain: the increased cost of freight (Cuba's main markets moved from 90 to 6,000 miles away); the higher costs paid on U.S. spare parts bought by Cuba through intermediaries (according to the Cubans the overprice ranges from 20 to 30 percent); the difficulties with shipping (Cuba's merchant marine carries only 7 to 8 percent of the island's trade); the relatively poor assortment and low quality of goods in Eastern Europe (as compared with the United States); and the higher price the Cubans pay for their imports from the Soviet bloc.[49] But Cuba is capable of selling all that it produces (actually the problem is that it does not produce enough) and of buying practically everything that the island needs either from socialist or market-economy countries. The embargo, instead, has provided the Cubans with an excuse for their poor economic performance and a propaganda tool for despising the

United States as a superpower strangling a small nation. Dropping an economically unoperative embargo would probably result in an improved political image of the United States abroad. The fourth condition is for the United States to get out of Guantánamo. This naval base, according to the opinion of military experts, does not have strategic significance today and is not really necessary to the United States. Its doubtful psychological value ("in spite of Castro we are still there") is offset by the risks of a grave incident that it constantly poses. (Castro seems to have placed a low priority on this condition; he attributed less importance to it in December 1972, although reconfirming it on May 1, 1973. Hence this condition may be negotiable.)

An American yielding to most of the Cuban conditions could be interpreted as a calamitous defeat. Conversely, the U.S. position could be presented as that of a great nation which has taken the initiative in removing a point of friction in the world, thus enhancing its own image and eliminating that of an encircled but challenging neighbor. The example of China proves that taking a noble initiative pays well in terms of both domestic and world opinion. There would also be more tangible benefits for the United States as a result of this normalization, such as the elimination of incidents between the two countries that could precipitate a grave confrontation.

The United States or Cuba: Who Is to Take the First Step?

At this point both the United States and Cuba are waiting for the other to make an overture; the question is who can afford to wait longer. Dr. Kissinger said, prior to the U.S. presidential election in 1972, that if Nixon were reelected, then the normalization of relations with Cuba would be "on the agenda." In the confirmation hearings of Kissinger before the Senate, held in September 1973, the new Secretary of State indicated that the United States would consult with Latin American countries as to whether the time had come for a relaxation of the hemispheric embargo of Cuba. Since then Kissinger has indicated his intention to solve the problem of relations with Cuba, through statements by official spokesmen and messages through third parties (e.g., Mexico and the U.S.S.R.)[50] It has also been reported that, by the end of 1973, three senators of the Foreign Relations Committee were told by Kissinger that in 1974 he planned to ask Congress to repeal the sanctions against Cuba.[51] In early 1974 there were rumors that Brezhnev had personally conveyed a message from Kissinger to Castro, and that Gromyko's direct flight from Havana to Washington was in part to discuss this matter with Nixon and Kissinger (Gromyko denied the rumor, however).[52] At that time Kissinger indicated that the United States had dropped its demand that Cuba cut military ties with the U.S.S.R. and that payment of compensation for confiscated U.S. property was not a precondition for lifting the embargo.[53] The inter-American conference of foreign ministers held in Mexico in 1974, in which Kissinger played an important role, declared that in the future, inter-American relationships will be based on non-intervention, renunciation of the use of force and coercion, and on the "respect for the right of countries to choose their own political, economic, and social system."[54] Soon after this conference, the U.S. government authorized the American subsidiaries of motor vehicles in Argentina to export cars and trucks to Cuba. This was followed by the vote of the inter-American conference of foreign ministers, held in Washington, to invite Cuba to the next meeting in Buenos Aires in 1975. Kissinger cautiously responded asking only a pooling of OAS members on the subject.

On the other side, although Castro repeatedly stated in 1971–1972 that neither Nixon nor Kissinger would visit Havana, he left the door open to negotiation by establishing his conditions and repeating them on various occasions. In January 1974, the Cuban Ambassador to Mexico, Fernando López Muiño, stated in a press interview that his country was not waging a holy war against the United States, that in spite of the military coup in Chile the "imperialists" had begun to change, and that Cuba was willing to meet with other Latin American countries to discuss common problems. (He said that the conference of foreign ministers in Mexico was a "valid attempt" to solve such problems and that Cuba was not attending it because it had not been invited.) López added that the only precondition to talks with the United States was the latter's unilateral lifting of its

economic embargo against Cuba. The restoration of the Guantánamo
base to Cuba was not mentioned by him as a precondition for
negotiations. Although later López declared that his words had been
misinterpreted and the Cuban Foreign Ministry issued a statement
reaffirming the old set of conditions, it was generally assumed that
the López incident was a balloon launched by Cuba.[55] In mid-1974
Castro changed his previous stand, announcing that he would meet
with Kissinger (a "realistic politician" as he put it) provided that the
United States would lift its embargo against Cuba.

Personal animosity between Castro and Nixon was often pointed
out as an obstacle to rapprochement. The former commonly
deprecated the latter as a "war criminal" and a "fascist," and the
Cuban press exacerbated the issue by systematically spelling Nixon's
name with a swastika (instead of an x) and ridiculing the American
president in political cartoons. Nixon, in turn, showed his personal
dislike of Castro as early as 1959, when he was vice-president, and
this feeling—reportedly—was kept afloat by his intimate friend
Charles ("Bebe") Rebozo, the son of Cuban immigrants, and Nixon's
Cuban-born valet. In August 1974, however, that obstacle was
removed by Nixon's resignation and his substitution by Gerald Ford.
Both the American president and the Cuban prime minister now face
internal and external forces that could move them rapidly toward
rapprochement.

Internally, the U.S. Congress will probably play a more active role
in revising relations with Cuba than under Nixon's presidency. In
that period U.S. Congressmen, such as Senators Fulbright, Hughes,
and Kennedy, unsuccessfully urged a revision of the U.S. policy
toward Cuba. In April 1972 a "Congressional Conference on
U.S.-Cuban Relations" took place in the Senate sponsored by thirty
senators (all Democrats except three) and with a team of fifteen
specialists debating the main issues. The conference was intended for
information rather than action; thus, it did not make any specific
recommendations although it was positive toward a normalization of
relations with Cuba (measures suggested were: ending the embargo
and travel restrictions; reestablishing commercial flights; and promoting the exchange of publications, scholars, newsmen, athletes, and
artists).[56] After the anti-hijacking agreement was signed, a group of

Republican Congressmen called for a dialogue with Cuba that could lead to an eventual normalization of relations between the two nations "in the interest of the U.S."[57] In July 1974, the Senate Foreign Relations Committee, presided over by William Fulbright, sent its Chief of Staff, Pat Holt, to Cuba with the authorization of the State Department. He met Castro and, on his return, advocated the reestablishment of relations with Cuba. The Committee is going to hold hearings to review the Cuban issue and will eventually make recommendations to the Congress and President Ford. It seems that the latter, confronting grave and urgent problems at home, will improve the relations of the Executive with the Congress and depend on Kissinger for his foreign policy.

Externally, the U.S. position has been strengthened on the one hand but weakened on the other. In the last decade, the increasing Soviet influence over Cuba has not recreated any internal security problems for the United States and conversely has helped to moderate the island's foreign policy. Sad as it is, the United States is better off dealing with a Soviet-dependent Castro than with him loose. Finally the anti-hijacking agreement has helped in dramatically reducing two frequent sources of tension: diversion of U.S. aircraft to Cuba and attacks of exiles against Cuban territory and vessels. (In October 1973, however, two Cuban fishing ships were attacked and burned, apparently by Cuban exiles.) On the other hand while Castro has become more peaceful and dependent on the U.S.S.R., his Latin American brothers have behaved in a more independent manner vis-a-vis the United States and presented a challenge to the latter on numerous fronts. In mid-1972 only two Latin American countries had relations with Cuba, but a year and a half later the number had risen to eight and three other countries were expected to follow the same path soon. The political changes in Chile and Venezuela modified the situation somewhat. Thus, in mid-1974, the likelihood was that the U.S. would not have to face an immediate challenge on Cuba at the OAS (similar to that of China at the UN). And yet the unstable political situation in Latin America makes it difficult to believe that the problem could be postponed too long. The pressures from the Latin American countries which are in favor of a rapprochement, the crisis in the OAS, and Kissinger's influence (who may concentrate on the Cuban issue in an attempt to emulate his past foreign policy achievements), are important factors that may move President Ford into taking the initiative.

Castro appears to also be in a weak internal position in view of the erosion of his charisma and the challenge to his power by internal forces led by Rodríguez and supported by the U.S.S.R. These forces give priority to the island's domestic problems and are in favor of the institutionalization of the Revolution and the normalization of Cuba's status in the Western Hemisphere. Economically, Cuba is doing poorly but has been able to survive the embargo, and the new economic policy and agreements with the U.S.S.R. will help. The reestablishment of trade with the United States would ease the burdens of the country but is not sufficient stimulus to induce Castro to an agreement. Normalization of relations with the United States would be a way to achieve more independence for Cuba but would doubtfully result in enlarged power for Castro if the United States and the U.S.S.R. had already reached an understanding. There is another way to look at the problem; this is that in the past Castro has exploited the real or imagined encirclement by the United States to his own advantage—as a scapegoat for the frequent mistakes of his administration and as a phantom to keep his forces united and to impose his personalistic-autocratic will. Castro's record shows that, whenever there has been a choice between his country's independence and his own power, he has sacrificed the first for his own gain. His provocative statements are indications of his concern about losing power, while his setting of conditions for negotiation is probably a result of Soviet pressure on him. Thus it is safe to predict that he will take the initiative in the negotiations only if he perceives that resisting Soviet pressure for normalization would erode his power even more. In view of the current state of Soviet-Cuban and U.S.-Soviet relations it is unrealistic for the United States to ask Castro (even if full guarantees are given to him to preserve his power and the socialist system on the island) to cut his ties with the Soviets and become totally independent. Between the two extremes (full Sovietization and total independence) lies a broad field for negotiation and the U.S. initiative could be critical in the outcome.

The U.S. policy of isolation of Cuba and wait-and-see, practiced in the last decade, has allowed increasing Sovietization and totalitarianism of the Cuban Revolution with the consequent curtailment of political and individual freedoms and the disappearance of the autochthonous characteristics of the Cuban process. The initial American-manifested concern over the negative domestic features of the Cuban regime (be it rhetorical or real) has been totally displaced by U.S. interests in external affairs. The normalization of American-Cuban relations could help to gain some independence for the island and perhaps more freedom and less economic hardships for its people. These results are by no means assured beforehand but would largely depend on the attitude and concerns of the United States. If it decides to take the initiative and does not neglect the interests of the Cuban people at the bargaining table, it may induce the slow transformation of the current centralist-dogmatic and Soviet-dependent Cuban regime into a more democratic and independent socialist system. In an era of realpolitik, this may be considered a rather naïve and romantic suggestion with which to close this chapter, but not for those who dream of a better world for tomorrow.

5

An Analysis of the Past
and a Forecast of the Future

The previous four chapters of this book have described the transformation that took place in Cuba in the 1970s and suggested some of the factors behind it. The first section of this chapter analytically illustrates the interrelation among those changes and better identifies their causes. For that purpose, a model that coherently integrates the most significant features of socialist systems is applied to Cuba at different points of its socialist history. Comparisons are also made between the Cuban and Soviet systems both in 1968 and 1973. The causes of the Cuban transformation of the 1970s and the alternatives that the country may have had are discussed here too. The second section of the chapter attempts to forecast how various features of the Cuban system will behave in the second half of the 1970s. This is done by contrasting the features of the Cuban and Soviet systems in 1973 and by assuming that the current trend reducing differences between the two will continue. Finally internal and external factors that may either support or impede such an approximation are evaluated.

An Attempt at Integration and Analysis

It is my contention that the changes that have taken place in several facets of the Cuban system (i.e., the economy, the government, the society, foreign relations) are not independent from each other and have not been generated by separate and disconnected causes but that those changes are interrelated and have been induced by a set of connected forces. To discuss these hypotheses and test them, we will use a model that I previously designed to compare and interrelate the most significant socio-politico-economic features of socialist systems.[1] (See Table 7.)

This model is a continuum divided into two fields by a "center" with two opposite "poles": X (positive) and Y (negative). Each of the

TABLE 7

A Static Comparison of Socialist Systems in Mid-1968

Predominance of:	Pole X	China	Cuba	Center	USSR	Czech.	Yugos	Pole Y
1. concentration of a clique over separation of gov't functions	2	2	2	0	-1	-2	-1	-2
2. mobilization over institutionalization	2	2	2	0	-2	-1	-1	-2
3. military over party power	2	2	2	0	-1	-2	-2	-2
4. rigidity over flexibility in cultural expression	2	2	0	0	1	-2	-2	-2
5. centralized over decentralized planning	2	1	0	0	1	-1	-2	-2
6. state administrator over self-management	2	0	2	0	1	0	-2	-2
7. loyalty over expertise in selection of managers	2	2	2	0	0	-1	-1	-2
8. communes and state farms over collective and private farms	2	2	1	0	0	0	-2	-2
9. utopian over realistic output targets	2	2	2	0	0	-1	-1	-2
10. capital accumulation over consumption	2	2	2	0	1	0	-1	-2
11. budgetary finance over self finance	2	0	2	0	0	-1	-2	-2
12. moral over material incentives	2	2	2	0	-1	-2	-2	-2
13. equality over stratification	2	2	2	0	-1	-1	-2	-2
14. full employment over high labor productivity	2	2	2	0	1	-1	-2	-2
15. isolation over integration with outside world	2	2	2	0	-1	-1	-2	-2
16. commitment to world revolution over coexistence	2	2	2	0	0	-2	-2	-2
TOTALS	32	27	27	0	-2	-18	-27	-32

Sources: Based on Carmelo Mesa-Lago, "A Continuum Model to Compare Socialist Systems Globally," *Economic Development and Cultural Change*, 21 (July 1973), pp. 573-90.

poles represents an ideal system abstracted from reality and its features are described by sixteen pairs of opposing variables (e.g., variable 1 in pole X is concentration of government functions in a clique, while in pole Y it is separation of government functions). Pole X is mainly (but not exclusively) characterized by emphasis on ideological development (the goals of a "New Man," world revolution, etc.), a mobilization regime, and anti-market tendencies. It is represented in reality by a few countries (e.g., China, Cuba) that at certain periods of their history have attempted to skip the socialist, transitional stage of evolution (or at least pass rapidly through it) and enter directly into a communist society. Pole Y is predominantly characterized by emphasis on material development (pragmatic goal as opposed to idealistic goal), institutionalization of politico-administrative processes, and market-oriented tendencies. It is represented in reality by countries (e.g., Yugoslavia) which have accepted the need for a transitional stage and temporarily postponed the ultimate goal of a communist society.

The comparison is static in time (mid–1968) because each of the countries selected has gone through important changes since socialism was introduced in them. Some of these countries have moved in a linear direction (e.g., Yugoslavia) while others in a cyclical manner (e.g., China). Therefore it is inappropriate to refer to "a system" in one country regardless of the time period. The Soviet system of War Communism (1918–1920), for instance, is different from Lenin's New Economic Policy (1921–1928), from the Stalinist era (1929–1953), and from the Economic-Reform system (1965 on). On the other hand the Chinese, Cuban, Czech, and Yugoslav systems during the early years of the first long-range plans had many features in common with the Stalinist system. The Cuban Sino-Guevarist system (1966–1970) at its peak in the 1968 "Revolutionary Offensive" showed strong similarity to the Chinese system of the "Great Leap Forward" (GLF) (1958–1960) and the "Great Proletarian Cultural Revolution" (GPCR) (1966–1968). The year 1968 was chosen for the comparison since by the middle of that year most of the countries in the model had reached a peak in the evolution of a stage, thereafter changing the direction or velocity of the movement.

The sixteen variables selected in the model embrace the most distinctive features among systems, hence similar features for all systems (e.g., collectivization of industry) are excluded. Variables have been qualitatively evaluated (based on published information on the five countries and a ranking made by some twenty specialists) rather than quantitatively measured. The set of variables evaluate the polarization of each system in relation to pole X with a five-point scale: 2 = very strong; 1 = strong; 0 = medium; -1 = weak; and -2 = very weak. The total score of a system places it in an appropriate position in the continuum. (The five countries in the model were selected for the comparison because, in 1968, they stood up as the best representatives of the poles and the center.) The ranking of sixteen "very strong" (a total of 32 points) is only achieved in the ideal system represented by pole X which is approximated in reality by the Chinese and Cuban systems. Conversely a ranking of sixteen "very weak" (a sum of -32) is only achieved in the ideal system represented by pole Y and approximated by Yugoslavia and, to a lesser extent, by Czechoslovakia. A ranking of sixteen "medium" (a total of zero) would describe the perfect center position, with the Soviet Union close to it but leaning toward pole Y. Each set of variables in the ideal systems at the poles of the continuum has internal cohesiveness. Variables in a real system have relative cohesiveness; that is, they tend to reinforce each other and to move in the same direction.[2]

The model shows how far apart Cuba and the U.S.S.R. were in mid–1968. The former had a ranking of 27, was in the same position as China, and was rapidly approximating pole X. The U.S.S.R. had a ranking of -2 and was slowly departing from the center toward pole Y. Cuba had fourteen variables ranked as very strong, one as strong, two as medium, and none as weak or very weak. Conversely the U.S.S.R. had six variables ranked as very weak or weak, five as medium, five as strong, and none as very strong. There were 29 points between the two systems.

In table 8, the same continuum model is used but to simplify it the poles and the center have been deleted. In addition, the comparison in table 7 is static while in table 8 it is dynamic. The latter traces the evolution of the Cuban system since socialism was introduced in 1961, at the peak of four stages: 1962 for the introduction of features

of the Stalinist Soviet system; 1965 for the experimentation with
opposing systems (Chinese of the GLF versus Soviet of the
Economic-Reform system); 1968 for the adoption of Sino-Guevarism
(an adaptation by Guevara and Castro to Cuba of the Chinese system
of the GLF and the GPCR); and 1973 for the movement toward the
Soviet Economic-Reform system. The Cuban variables evaluated in
table 8 roughly correspond with those features summarized in
chapter 1, table 1, although in the latter they were ordered
differently.

Table 8 clearly indicates that in 1962–1965 Cuba was moving
toward the center thus approximating the Soviet position. As a result
of the 1961–1963 attempt to apply the Stalinist system to Cuba,
central planning was introduced, there was a reversion in the
previous consumptionist policy (1959–1960) to increase capital
accumulation, the budgetary system of finance was organized in the
recently collectivized state sector, and full employment was
achieved. But autochthonous features of the Cuban Revolution were
still salient: charismatic leadership, mobilization, predominance of
the army (the ORI organized in 1961 was controlled by the
Castroites in 1962), and the guerrilla mentality shown in utopian
output targets, distaste for technicians, egalitarianism, and strong
commitment to continental revolution. In 1964–1965 Cuba moved
closer to the U.S.S.R. by the partial introduction in the former of
some of the economic reforms that had been tested in the latter, such
as self-financing and decentralization techniques which also resulted
in more realistic output targets in certain sectors of the economy. In
addition, the PCC was established and there was a temporary
compromise with pro-Soviet Communist parties in selected Latin
American countries to play down guerrilla warfare in them.

But in 1966 the adoption of Sino-Guevarism generated a dramatic
shift in the opposite direction: Castro became the undisputed
ideologist of the Revolution (after Rodríguez's dismissal and Guevara's departure), mobilization was accentuated while several institutions declined (e.g., the party, the unions, JUCEPLAN), the army
expanded its influence enormously, several journals that had participated in the controversy over alternative systems were closed down
(steps against deviant intellectuals were taken), planning remained

TABLE 8

A Dynamic Comparison of the Cuban System at the Peak of Each Stage and with the Soviet System in 1973

Predominance of:	Cuba				USSR
	1962	*1965*	*1968*	*1973*	*1973*
1. concentration on a clique over separation of gov't functions	2	1	2	0	-1
2. mobilization over institutionalization	2	1	2	0	-2
3. military over party power	2	2	2	1	-1
4. rigidity over flexibility in cultural expression	-1	-1	0	1	1
5. centralized over decentralized planning	1	0	0	1	1
6. state administrator over self-management	2	2	2	1	1
7. loyalty over expertise in selection of managers	1	1	2	0	0
8. communes and state farms over collective and private farms	1	1	1	1	0
9. utopian over realistic output targets	1	0	2	0	0
10. capital accumulation over consumption	1	1	2	1	1
11. budgetary finance over self finance	2	1	2	1	0
12. moral over material incentives	-1	-1	2	-1	-1
13. equality over stratification	1	1	2	0	-1
14. full employment over high labor productivity	2	1	2	1	1
15. isolation over integration with outside world	1	2	2	-1	-2
16. commitment to world revolution over coexistence	2	1	2	0	-1
TOTALS	20	13	27	6	-4

Sources: Based on Chapter I, table 1 and other data scattered in this book.

centralized but became politicized in decision making (mini or sectorial plans were substituted for macro-national plans also), grandiose sugar output targets were set up, capital accumulation grew to be an obsession, self-financing was eradicated, moral incentives and egalitarianism were vigorously expanded in the pursuit of the "New Man," work quotas declined and labor productivity was completely disregarded, and the exportation of the Revolution took momentum.

The climax of the Cuban movement away from the U.S.S.R. and toward pole X occurred in the first half of 1968. Nevertheless, the death of Che Guevara a few months before had sealed the fate of the exportation of the Revolution, and Castro's endorsement of the Soviet invasion of Czechoslovakia in August put in motion the shift in Cuban foreign policy (variables 15 and 16): accommodation with the U.S.S.R. and a more moderate attitude toward Latin America in order to break the island's isolation. In spite of these external changes, the domestic policy of Cuba (represented by variables 1 through 14) remained unchanged until 1970. The economic dislocation created by the sugar harvest failure proved the unfeasibility of the development strategy and the necessary foundation for building the "New Man" collapsed. The Cuban debt with the U.S.S.R. was astronomical and to get the nation out of the abyss in which it had fallen massive aid and viable economic strategy and organization were desperately needed. The U.S.S.R. was willing to postpone the debt payments, to grant more credit and technical help, and to increase the price paid for Cuban exports on the condition that such aid would be used rationally and that Cuba would honor its export commitments. That meant that the Cuban system had to be transformed into the Soviet image. Castro accepted the deal as evidenced by Cuba's dramatic shift to the center of the continuum shown for 1973 in table 8: delegation of Castro's power and separation of government functions (rise of old members of PSP to top positions); decline in mobilization and move to institutionalization; development of the party; tightening of controls in ideology, culture and education; reintroduction of macro-, long-run technical planning; revitalization of the unions with potential to make suggestions in production issues; stress on managerial skills; setting up of rational output targets, especially in sugar; reduction of the investment rate with a parallel increase in capital efficiency; the probable reintroduction of self-financing; the return to material incentives; the justification of wage differentials; the concern over labor productivity and acknowledgement of the appearance of unemployment pockets; the proclamation of total unity of ideas between Cuba and the U.S.S.R. with the former becoming the unconditional defender of the latter in the Third World; the breaking of Cuba's isolation by reestablishment of diplomatic and/or trade relations with a dozen Latin American countries and the halt in the exportation of the Revolution; the setting up of conditions for negotiation with the United States and the beginning of an acceptance—even if reluctantly—of peaceful coexistence. While in 1968 Cuba was close to pole X and separated by 29 points from the U.S.S.R. in the continuum, in 1973 Cuba was close to the center and only 10 points apart from the U.S.S.R. Between 1968 and 1973 Cuba moved 21 points to the right in the continuum. (See the last two columns of table 8 which compare the Cuban and Soviet systems in 1973.)

The question could be raised if Cuba, facing defeat in both the external and internal fronts (death of Guevara in 1967 and economic dislocation in 1970), had no other alternative but to yield to Soviet pressure. In trying to answer that question a brief review of the peculiarities of Cuba is necessary.[3] It is an island lacking many vital resources, with a low degree of development, and it has traditionally been economically dependent on a foreign power. The main source of Cuban foreign exchange is still sugar (about 80 percent of its exports) and, to a lesser extent, tobacco and nickel. The country lacks basic energy sources (oil, coal, or rivers with strong currents) and has to import about 98 percent of the oil that it needs. The industrial base is very small (basically U.S. or Soviet made) and heavily dependent on imported inputs and spare parts, as well as foreign technical aid. Most manufactured products have to be imported. In spite of good physical conditions and the expansion of the agricultural infrastructure, planning errors, incorrect incentives, climatological factors (hurricanes and drought), and the excessive concentration on sugar have impeded self sufficiency in food and maintained a high proportion of imports of foodstuffs.

At the beginning of the 1960s the U.S.S.R. replaced the United States as the supplier of capital, intermediate and manufactured goods, as well as oil and foodstuffs in exchange for Cuban sugar and other raw materials. The inability of Cuba to expand its exports and the small degree of import substitution resulted in a growing deficit in the balance of payments with the U.S.S.R. Such deficits were mostly covered with Soviet credit; the Cuban foreign debt with the U.S.S.R. in 1970 had risen above $3 billion (equivalent to the Cuban average annual GNP during the 1960s). The possibility of shifting the direction of trade and external financing to the Western Hemisphere was nil in the 1960s due to the breaking of trade and diplomatic relations with all countries except Canada and Mexico. China's aid in the first half of the 1960s was small and the confrontation of this country with Cuba in 1965 resulted in a subsequent sharp decline in trade between the two. In spite of the similarities of the Cuban and Chinese systems in 1966–1968 there was no significant interaction between the two countries. China was seriously handicapped at the end of that period by the internal turmoil caused by the Cultural Revolution. Western Europe and Japan did not open large lines of credit to Cuba because they knew of the island's poor capacity for repayment and did not want to alienate the United States. Third World countries were either not independent, not interested, and/or not powerful enough to come to Cuba's aid; the Arab world in particular was in disarray after their calamitous defeat in the 1967 war against Israel.

The development strategy based on steady gigantic sugar crops in the 1970s could, in theory, have generated a large surplus to gradually repay the debt to the U.S.S.R., expand trade with capitalist countries, and allow Cuba to increase its independence. The feasibility of such a strategy, however, was not a subject of a serious prior analysis but largely the personal decision of Castro. He became totally and directly involved in the sugar plan, played his last card in 1970, and lost the battle. The difference between final output (8.5 million tons) and the target (10 million) was precisely the surplus that

Cuba needed (after satisfying internal consumption and export commitments) to begin reducing the foreign debt. Furthermore the chances of repeating a harvest above 7 million tons in the 1970s were zero. During the second half of the 1960s the Cuban masses had been promised again and again that the sugar target would be fulfilled and that their sacrifices would be rewarded with a better life in the 1970s. Thus the failure to reach the goal was a psychological blow aggravated by the decline in production in the non-sugar sector. Discontent, skepticism, and withdrawal of the labor force were the visible results. Castro's prestige was severely damaged and his charisma—as a unifying force in the Revolution—was eroded.

The United States could have played a crucial role in that juncture by associating with Mexico, Chile, and Peru in lifting economic sanctions against Cuba, facilitating her reintegration into the Western Hemisphere, and offering an alternative to Cuba vis-a-vis the U.S.S.R. There is evidence that some consideration was given to this strategy in influential circles of the U.S. government. (For example, a sophisticated study conducted at Rand Corporation in early 1971 made a computerized analysis of several Cuban leaders ranking them according to their stand in numerous issues and their proclivity to a potential rapprochement.[4]) And yet at that time Nixon was working out the preliminary details for the détente with the U.S.S.R. and any movement to "neutralize" Cuba would have seriously hampered his strategy. For the United States, détente with the Soviet Union had a much higher priority than neutralization of Cuba. Finally the Americans could easily foresee that increased Soviet control over Cuba would retain the economic burden upon Soviet shoulders (instead of upon the United States) and reduce the exportation of the Revolution to Latin America.

The continuation of the Sino-Guevarist system was not feasible. Economically it would have deteriorated the situation even more without any serious hope of eventual improvement. Politically it would have dangerously exacerbated the discontent among the masses, created the preconditions for a grave conflict or upsurge (such as the ones which occurred in Germany, Hungary, and Poland in the 1950s) and eventually destroyed the remnants of support behind Castro. The possibility of a compromise, making some economic changes to immediately alleviate the situation of the masses (e.g., increase in consumption, decline in voluntary labor) but retaining other features of the Cuban system, had to be ruled out because it would have required substantial economic aid from outside Eastern Europe (e.g., the United States) which was not available. It seems, therefore, that the only real alternative open to Castro was to yield to the Soviets. He would have to relinquish part of his power and Cuba its independence but he and the Revolution would continue.

A Forecast for the Remainder of the 1970s

Let us start with the assumptions that, for the remainder of the 1970s, the current Soviet influence over Cuba will continue and that the Economic-Reform Soviet system will remain basically unchanged. Based on these two premises, it can be predicted that Cuba will proceed in its movement toward the center of the continuum and close the gap with the U.S.S.R. Using the knowledge accumulated in the previous four chapters and the two columns of table 8, a cautious forecast can be made of the behavior of the sixteen features of the Cuban system in the rest of the 1970s.

There will be a continuation in the separation of government functions and the delegation of Castro's power. The prime minister will probably devote more time to foreign trips and less to domestic technical issues such as economic decision making. The trends of declining mobilization and increasing institutionalization will proceed. The new political constitution and civil code will be enacted. The PCC will expand its membership and possibly augment the proportion of workers in its ranks. The PCC congress will be held and the party program and bylaws promulgated. In the congress elections, former members of the PSP and younger technocrats will likely gain more positions, and there is the possibility that Castro will relinquish his job as first secretary general. The party prestige and influence will rise approximating that of the army. The latter will be basically limited to military functions. There will be an expansion in the membership of most mass organizations except the ANAP.

Unions will remain active but their main role will abide as transmission belts of the administration. Rigidity in cultural expression will endure, although increasing communication with the outside world (especially Latin America and probably the United States) may generate an opposite tendency in favor of flexibility.

The strengthening of central planning with computers, more accurate statistics and technicians will take momentum with the implementation of the first five-year plan in 1976–1980. There will probably be a resumption of the publication of important statistical series, e.g., on national accounts, employment, and wages. Administrators in state enterprises will retain decision-making authority although unions' and workers' suggestions in production matters will probably receive more attention. It is difficult to predict what will happen to the "organs of popular power" if they are nationally implemented. Emphasis in skills will be maintained, with a growing number of graduates in accounting, economics, and technological careers (many of them studying in the U.S.S.R.) and gradual substitution of technocrats for political cadres (or the latter raising their skills). Private agriculture will shrink even more due to deaths of private farmers, state purchases, expansion of *acopio,* and reduction of wage earners employed in this sector.

Caution and realism in fixing output targets will be entrenched. GNP will probably grow at a modest but steady rate of from 5 to 6 percent annually or from 3 to 4 percent per capita. The modern industrial sector, nickel, fishing, and mechanized agriculture will steadily increase their output. Sugar harvests will yield from 5 to 6 million tons. If the KTP-1 harvest combines are produced on schedule (and fulfill expectations in efficiency) and the Australian method is mastered, sugar crops will gradually rise. Results in the rest of agriculture will be ambiguous. The reduction in private agriculture and the lack of adequate incentives to the farmers will be negative factors in terms of output and efficiency. Investment rates will likely be set at about 22 to 24 percent of GNP. Consumption of manufactured products will increase and, if mechanization of sugar materializes and sugar prices remain high, there should be some reduction in rationing of foodstuffs (through an increase in imports). Chances are that self-financing will be reintroduced in some sectors of the economy (e.g., agriculture, foreign trade) bringing credit and interest back to the Cuban economy. An attempt will be made to improve budgetary financing (either in all of the economy if self-financing is not reintroduced or in most of it) with techniques from both a command economy (e.g., the "economic file," an improved pay-off formula for more efficient capital allocation) or a market economy (e.g., profit as an important indicator of managerial performance). The price system will be the subject of study and, perhaps, of reform to make prices better allocators.

Material incentives will keep up and tie closer to labor skills and productivity. The equilibrium between population income and consumer goods will be improved further by reducing the monetary surplus to a manageable amount. Inequality will probably increase through expansion of wage differentials, substitution of prices for rationing, and freezing (or perhaps reduction) of available free social services. Work quotas will become more technically fixed in industry thereby helping to improve labor productivity but still facing serious difficulties in non-mechanized agriculture. Production bonuses will hold on while the use of voluntary labor and overtime may decline if the labor surplus grows. Also if unemployment pockets become more frequent, there may be an attempt to introduce family planning and/or to export the labor surplus, possibly to the United States.

A majority of Latin American countries will reestablish diplomatic and/or trade relations with Cuba, among them probably Venezuela, Panama, Ecuador, and Colombia. Exchange of visits of chiefs of state between Cuba and other Latin American and socialist countries will be frequent. Although it is not likely that Cuba will return to the OAS (unless it is dramatically reformed), the former will become integrated with several hemispheric institutions, some of them linked to the OAS. A rapprochement between Cuba and the United States will take place, probably initiated by an agreement within the OAS or an inter-American conference of foreign ministers, to lift the economic sanctions against Cuba. If the American-Soviet détente continues, normalization of U.S.-Cuban relations will not result in the "neutralization" of Cuba but will give greater flexibility to the latter in trade, credit, oil, and spare-part supplies, and reduce its freight costs. The degree of resumption of economic relations with the United States will largely determine the degree of dependence of Cuba upon the U.S.S.R. and Comecon. The exportation of the Revolution will come to a halt and peaceful coexistence will be gradually accepted by Cuba.

Let me now discuss some external and internal factors that may affect Soviet influence over Cuba and indirectly the accuracy of the previous forecast. In order to reduce dependency on the Soviets, Cuba would have to find alternative sources for credit, oil, and military aid as well as trade partners capable of substituting for the U.S.S.R. We have already seen that this possibility is a poor one. Due to the American-Soviet détente and the Cubans' distrust of the United States, it is not likely that the latter will substitute for the U.S.S.R. significantly. And yet without promoting Cuban total independence from the U.S.S.R., the United States can help to reduce the island's current degree of dependency on the Soviets. An American-Cuban relationship, however, will tend to move Cuba toward pole Y, which is to say in the same direction in which it is being pushed by the U.S.S.R. And yet, there could be important differences in some variables, for instance, in the matter of flexibility in cultural expression. We have ruled out the possibility of China taking the place of the U.S.S.R. and hence of reversing the current movement of Cuba. The Arab countries could substitute for the Soviets in oil but not in capital equipment, military aid, and other vital supplies. Western Europe has the potential but not the interest to take up the Soviet role. Chile's military coup, reformism in Peru, and conservatism in Argentina have practically eliminated the possibility of a grouping of socialist countries in Latin America which could integrate an anti-U.S. axis and act as a bargaining agent with the U.S.S.R. In the present situation, Latin America does not have the resources and willingness to substitute for the U.S.S.R. and is busy trying to make agreements with the United States, taking advantage of the high prices of raw materials.[5]

Internally, even if the predicted economic recuperation of Cuba materializes, it will not be significant enough to reduce dependency on the Soviets to any noticeable degree. Besides, Castro's power has declined and he no longer enjoys the capacity for maneuver that he had in the 1960s. Both the pro-Soviet group and the young generation of technocrats have a vested interest in the current process of institutionalization, professionalization, and pragmatism. These are increasingly powerful forces that, in alliance with the U.S.S.R., may stop the prime minister in any attempt to turn back to mobilization, radicalization, and idealism. Castro himself, being a consummate politician, has probably learned by now that the only way that he can keep the remnants of his power is to hold the Revolution on its current path. Even if he is uncomfortable with his reduced role in the process, he is being induced to compromise due to the absence of a viable substitute for the Soviets. Unless something totally unexpected occurs, and this cannot be ruled out in politics, we should see Cuba moving in the direction forecast above for the rest of the decade.

Notes

CHAPTER 1

1. For details on the politico-economic-social aspects of the 1959–1970 stages, see the book edited by me, *Revolutionary Change in Cuba* (Pittsburgh: The University of Pittsburgh Press, 1971).

2. On the 1963–1966 debate see Bertram Silverman, *Man and Socialism in Cuba: The Great Debate* (New York: Atheneum, 1971); Robert M. Bernardo, *The Theory of Moral Incentives in Cuba* (University, Alabama: The University of Alabama Press, 1971); and my articles "Ideological, Political and Economic Factors in the Cuban Controversy on Material Versus Moral Incentives," *Journal of Interamerican Studies and World Affairs* 14 (February, 1972): 49–111, and "Revolutionary Morality?," *Society* 9 (July-August 1972): 70–76.

3. Little has been written on this new stage of the Revolution, mostly articles by Europeans: Charles Vanhecke, "Cuba: de l'utopie aux réalités," *Le Monde*, March 17–20, 1971; Charles Bettelheim, "La révolution cubaine sur la voie soviétique," *Le Monde*, May 12, 1971; Jacques Valier, "Cuba 1968–1971: le développement des déformations bureaucratiques et des difficultés économiques," *Critiques et L'Economie Politique*, No. 6 (January-March 1972); "Cuba: From Dogma to Pragmatism?" *Bolsa Review* (London), April 1972; and "Cuba: The New Realism," *Latin America* (London), May 19, 1972. See also Edward González, *Cuba Under Castro: The Limits of Charisma* (Boston: Houghton Mifflin Co., 1974), pp. 217–36. At the time that this book was entering the printing stage a well-documented and challenging essay by Andrés Suarez, partly discussing the new stage, came into my hands: "The Politics of Cuba Under Castro: How Socialist is Cuba?," paper delivered at the Meeting of the American Political Science Association, New Orleans, September 1973.

4. See K. S. Karol, *Guerrillas in Power: The Course of the Cuban Revolution* (New York: Hill & Wang, 1970); Edward González, "Relationship with the Soviet Union," *Revolutionary Change in Cuba*, pp. 81–104; Charles Bettelheim, "La révolution cubaine sur la voie soviétique"; and Leon Gouré and Julian Weinkle, "Cuba's New Dependency," *Problems of Communism* 21 (March-April 1972): 68–79.

5. Radio Moscow, transmissions of December 9, 1970, and February 22, 1971. The extension of the trade agreement was not reported by the Cuban press.

6. *Granma Weekly Review*, May 2 and 16, 1971, p. 12 and June 20 and 27, p. 1.

7. "Cuban-Soviet Commission for Economic, Scientific and Technical Collaboration Holds First Session," *Granma Weekly Review*, September 12, 1971, p. 7.

8. "Novikov and Carlos Rafael Rodríguez Sign Protocol of Collaboration between

Cuba and the USSR" (and in smaller print: "Prime Minister Castro Attends Signing"), *Granma Weekly Review*, September 19, 1971, p. 3.

9. Radio Moscow, transmission of September 25, 1971.

10. "Palabras en el Reparto Alamar," Instituto Cubano de Radiodifusión, transmission of October 27, 1971. See also the daily edition of *Granma*, October 25–30, 1971.

11. "Joint Soviet-Cuban Communique," *Granma Weekly Review*, November 7, 1971, p. 1.

12. *Granma Weekly Review*, January 9, 1972, p. 10.

13. See Marcel Niedergang, "La récent voyage de M. Fidel Castro a confirmé son alignement sur Moscou," *Le Monde Diplomatique*, August 1972; "Brazil, Sugar Challenge to Cuba," *Latin America* 2 (January 1972): 9–10; and "Inestabilidad del mercado azucarero," *Progreso* (August 1972): 35–76.

14. "Cordial Nixon-Mao Interview; Chou-Nixon Friendly Meeting; Paper Tiger Gives Syrupy Speech in Peking," *Granma Weekly Review*, February 27, 1972, pp. 1, 7, 12. See also ibid., March 5, 1972, pp. 1, 12. Chinese-Cuban relations reached a low ebb in January, 1974 when the New China News Agency excluded Cuba from the Latin American countries worthy of receiving socialist support. (Argentina, Ecuador, Mexico, Peru and Venezuela were the countries mentioned.)

15. "Sale Nixon en viaje a la URSS," *Granma*, May 17, 1972, p. 5; "Llegó Nixon a Moscú," ibid., May 23, p. 6; "Actividades de Nixon en Moscú," ibid., May 24, p. 5; "Llegó Nixon a Varsovia," *Granma*, June 1, p. 6; "Terminó Nixon su visita a Polonia," ibid., June 2, p. 7. The weekly editions of *Granma* did not publish news on the visit.

16. "Firman Cuba y la URSS protocolo de la segunda sesión de la Comisión Intergubernamental de Colaboración Económica y Científico-Técnica," *Granma*, April 17, 1972, p. 6. See also A. Voronov, "Soviet-Cuban Cooperation Enters New Stage," *International Affairs* (Moscow) (September 1972): 81.

17. Raúl Castro, "Speech at the Naval Parade on Revolutionary Navy Day," *Granma Weekly Review*, August 13, 1972, p. 5.

18. Radio Rebelde, transmission of April 18, 1972. See also *Granma Weekly Review*, April 23, 1972, p. 2.

19. F. Castro, "Speech at the May Day Parade and Workers' Rally," *Granma Weekly Review*, May 7, 1972, p. 5. Information on the trip comes from ibid., May-July editions and the Cuban radio. See also "Fidel por 10 países," *Cuba Internacional* 4 (September 1972): 4–71.

20. Until Cuba's entrance Comecon was composed of the seven Eastern European countries visited by Castro, plus Mongolia. Observers were Cuba, North Korea, North Vietnam, and Yugoslavia. In 1962, Albania was excluded. China neither entered Comecon nor sent observers.

21. C. R. Rodríguez, "Speech at the 26th Session of the Council for Mutual Economic Assistance," *Granma Weekly Review*, July 23, 1972, p. 10.

22. See for instance Gouré and Weinkle's opinion, "Cuba's New Dependency," p. 77, published three months before Cuba entered Comecon.

23. See Theodore Shabad, "Cuba Becomes Full Member of Soviet Economic Bloc," *The New York Times,* July 12, 1972, p. 2.

24. Boris Gorbachov, "Cuba: Algunas cuestiones de su integración económica con los países del socialismo," *Panorama Latinoamericano* (Moscow), No. 171 (August 1, 1973): 10–12.

25. Rodríguez has argued that statistical similarity could not hold in economic and political terms. See "Diálogo con Carlos Rafael Rodríguez," *Cuba Internacional* 3 (November-December 1971): 86–91.

26. See my chapter, "Economic Policies and Growth," *Revolutionary Change in Cuba,* pp. 301–303.

27. Soviet sources are: *Vneshniaia torgovlia SSSR: statisticheskii sbornik 1918-1966* and *Vneshniaia torgovlia SSSR za 1968 god* (Moscow: Mezhdunarodnie Otnosheniia, 1967 and 1969), pp. 69 and 15; *Foreign Trade* (Moscow), No. 6, 1970, p. 55, and No. 5, 1971, p. 48. Cuban sources are Junta Central de Planificación, *BE Boletín Estadístico 1970* (La Habana: JUCEPLAN, 1971), pp. 188–91. See also Eric N. Baklanoff, "International Economic Relations," *Revolutionary Change in Cuba,* pp. 258–76.

28. In 1971 the value of Soviet imports increased by 17 percent to a record 800 million pesos, while Cuban exports to the U.S.S.R. probably declined by 40 percent to 280 million pesos due to a decline in sugar production from 8.5 million tons in 1970 to 5.9 million tons in 1971. Probably the level of Soviet imports in 1972 remained equal while that of Cuban exports to the U.S.S.R. declined due to an even worse sugar crop. The 1971–1972 combined deficit was probably close to one billion pesos.

29. By Gouré and Weinkle, "Cuba's New Dependency," p. 75, without giving a clear source.

30. F. Castro, "Speech at the Main Event in Commemoration of the Victory of Playa Girón," *Granma Weekly Review,* May 2, 1971, p. 6.

31. Martin Schram, "Cuba Today: The Party Seeks Economic Revival," *Newsday,* September 13, 1971; and Gouré/Weinkle, "Cuba's New Dependency," p. 78. The Soviet official figure of its technicians in Cuba is of 1,000 only. See Gorbachov, "Cuba: Algunas cuestiones," p. 3.

32. *Granma Weekly Review,* February 17, 1974, p. 11.

33. See González, "Relationship with the Soviet Union," pp. 82–86.

34. F. Castro, "Speech on the 19th Anniversary of the Attack on the Moncada Garrison," *Granma Weekly Review,* August 6, 1972, pp. 3–6.

35. "Executive Committee of Council of Ministries Established," *Granma Weekly Review,* December 3, 1972, p. 2.

36. F. Castro, "Speech at the Solemn Session in Honor of the 50th Anniversary of the USSR," *Granma Weekly Review,* December 31, 1972, p. 9. Castro also said (p. 16) that he felt at home in Moscow and that a man could have two homelands.

37. F. Castro, "Report to the People on the Economic Agreements Signed with the Soviet Union," *Granma Weekly Review,* January 14, 1973, pp. 2–3.

38. "3rd Session of the Cuban-Soviet Intergovernmental Commission for Economic, Scientific and Technical Collaboration Opened," *Granma Weekly Review,* March 4, 1973, p. 3.

39. See *Granma Weekly Review*, March 25, 1973, pp. 4–5.

40. See Janette Habel, *Proceso al sectarismo* (Buenos Aires: Jorge Alvarez Editor, 1965).

41. *Granma Weekly Review*, April 15, 1973, p. 4.

42. F. Castro, "Speech Analyzing Events in Czechoslovakia," *Granma Weekly Review*, August 25, 1968, pp. 2–3.

43. TANJUG (Yugoslav News Agency), Belgrade, June 27, 1973.

44. F. Castro, "Speech Analyzing Events in Czechoslovakia," p. 3; and "Discurso en el séptimo aniversario de la derrota del imperialismo yanqui en Playa Girón," *Granma Resumen Semanal*, April 28, 1968, p. 6. Castro and Tito had a meeting during the Conference of Nonaligned Countries in Algiers which opened a "new stage of relations" between Cuba and Yugoslavia. In February 1974, a Cuban delegation led by Raúl Castro visited Yugoslavia, hailed Tito and the League of Communists, acknowledged Yugoslav achievements in the "construction of socialism," agreed to expand cooperation between the two countries, and invited Tito to visit Cuba. See *Granma Weekly Review*, March 3, 1974, pp. 10–11 and March 10, 1974, p. 11.

45. For a coverage of the trip see *Granma Weekly Review*, September 15, 23, and 30, 1973.

46. F. Castro, "Speech at the Fourth Conference of Nonaligned Nations," *Granma Weekly Review*, September 16, 1973, p. 12.

47. As quoted by George Volsky, "Cuba Fifteen Years Later," *Current History 66* (January 1974): 13.

48. "Cuba: Sentimental Journey," *Latin America* (January 4, 1974): 4–5.

49. As reported by TASS and transmitted by the Associated Press, January 29, 1974. For Western coverage of the visit see "Cuba: Brezhnev Visit" and "Cuba: The Russian Perspective," *Latin America* (February 1 and 8, 1974): 34–36, 46–47; and "Bienvenido Brezhnev," *Time* (February 11, 1974): 37–38.

50. Information on the visit discussed in this chapter comes from *Granma* and Cuban radio transmissions, January 26 through February 4. The January 29 issue of *Granma* was totally devoted to the visit.

51. Work on a two-way station satellite between Cuba and the U.S.S.R. began in December, 1970 by a Soviet team of thirty engineers. Three years later Cuba was incorporated into the Intersputnik System of Communications. The first direct television transmission, from Moscow to Havana, was the military parade held on November 7, 1973, in Red Square on the 56th anniversary of the Bolshevik Revolution. On January 2, 1974, the Cuban military parade commemorating the fifteenth anniversary of the Revolution was transmitted to Moscow. The transmission of Brezhnev's visit was the third. A final stage in the project will permit direct telephone and telegraph communication between the two countries. Cuba became thus linked with the U.S.S.R. before Eastern Europe. (Czechoslovakia and the GDR would be the first to be connected in 1974–1975.) "The Satellite Station in Cuba," *Granma Weekly Review*, January 20, 1974, p. 6.

52. F. Castro, "Discurso en la concentración popular en honor del compañero Brezhnev," *Granma*, January 30, 1974, pp. 2–3.

53. L. Brezhnev, "Discurso en la concentración popular," *Granma*, January 30, 1974, pp. 4–5.

54. "Declaración cubano-soviética," *Granma*, February 5, 1974. Cuban support for the Soviets' moves toward détente with the United States and international peace revised its former stand as expressed in 1968 by Castro's criticism of the socialist countries' "constant, foolish, and inexplicable campaign in favor of peace." Castro, "Speech Analyzing Events in Czechoslovakia," p. 2.

55. F. Castro, "Discurso en el X aniversario de la constitución de la FMC," *Granma Revista Semanal*, August 30, 1970, pp. 4–5.

56. F. Castro, "Speech at the Closing Session of the National Plenary Meeting of Basic Industry," *Granma Weekly Review*, December 20, 1970, pp. 2–3.

57. F. Castro, "Franco debate obrero sobre ausentismo y trabajo voluntario," *Granma*, September 8, 1970, p. 5.

58. F. Castro, "Speech at the Closing Session," p. 4.

59. F. Castro, "Speech in the Rally to Celebrate May Day," *Granma Weekly Review*, May 16, 1971, pp. 7–8.

60. F. Castro, "Speech to the Workers in Chuquicamata," *Granma Weekly Review*, November 28, 1971, p. 6; and Press Interview, *Granma Weekly Review*, December 19, 1971, pp. 12–13.

61. At the concluding session of the Cuban-Soviet Commission's first meeting, Rodríguez had stated that Cuba was "constructing socialism." Later, in the communiqué released on the occasion of Kosygin's visit, the Soviet side said that Cuba was "constructing the foundations of socialism." The importance of the Dorticós-Brezhnev statements is that they were made at Moscow, using the correct Russian terminology and, then, were reproduced in the Cuban press. See *Granma Weekly Review*, January 2, 1972, p. 12. On January 28, 1974, in an interview for Soviet television, Castro said in Havana: "In the U.S.S.R. a *new man* has been forged corresponding to a society that has built socialism and is constructing communism." (Emphasis is mine.)

62. See *Granma*, November 19, 1972, pp. 8–9. For a cautious review of the incentives controversy see interview with Carlos Rafael Rodríguez in *Economía y Desarrollo* No. 14 (November-December 1972): 149–53.

63. See as an example, Felipe Carneado, "Social Being and Social Consciousness," *Granma Weekly Review*, April 1, 1973, p. 2.

64. F. Castro, "Speech at the Main Ceremony Marking the 20th Anniversary of the Attack on the Moncada Garrison," *Granma Weekly Review*, August 5, 1973, p. 5. Contrary to his custom of improvising his speeches, Castro read this one from a written text.

65. F. Castro, "Discurso en el Acto de Clausura del XIII Congreso de la CTC," *Juventud Rebelde* (November 16, 1973): 2–11.

CHAPTER 2

1. For details on planning in the 1960s, see Carmelo Mesa-Lago and Luc Zephirin, "Central Planning," *Revolutionary Change in Cuba*, Mesa-Lago, ed., pp. 145–84.

2. W. Leontief, "Notes on a Visit to Cuba," *New York Review of Books* 13 (August 21, 1969): 16.

3. República de Cuba, Dirección Central de Estadística, *BE Boletín Estadístico 1966, 1968*, and *1970* (La Habana: JUCEPLAN, 1968, 1970, and 1971). It is expected that the next bulletin (for 1971–1972 to be published in 1974) will reintroduce macroeconomic indicators such as GMP growth, total wage bill, total state employment, and gross investment.

4. O. Dorticós, "Control económico y perspectivas del desarrollo de la economía cubana," *Economía y Desarrollo*, no. 11 (May-June 1972): 10, 27–28.

5. F. Castro, "Speech at the May Day Parade and Workers' Rally," *Granma Weekly Review*, May 7, 1972, p. 4.

6. Based on a statement by A. Kosygin quoted by *Granma Weekly Review*, July 23, 1972, p. 10.

7. "Franco debate obrero," *Granma*, September 8, 1970, p. 5.

8. See chapter 1.

9. Orlando Carnota, "La aplicación de las computadoras en el campo económico y social en un país en vías de desarrollo: Cuba," *Economía y Desarrollo*, no. 9 (January-February 1972): 84–129; "Cuba and the Computer," *Granma Weekly Review*, April 2, 1972, p. 5; Luis Gutiérrez, "El desarrollo de la computación electrónica en Cuba," *Economía y Desarrollo*, no. 12 (July-August 1972): 144–49; Osvaldo Dorticós, "Desarrollar cultural, científica y técnicamente los cuadros administrativos," *Economía y Desarrollo*, no. 20 (November-December 1973), pp. 27–57; and Ramon C. Barquín, "The State of Computation in Cuba," *Datamation Journal* (December 1973): 69–72.

10. Dorticós, "Control económico," pp. 30–31.

11. F. Castro, "Speech at Río Verde Sheep Farm, Magallanes," *Granma Weekly Review*, December 5, 1971, p. 8.

12. F. Castro, "Discurso en la inauguración del primer edificio del Plan de Participación Masiva en las Construcciones," transmitted by Radio Havana, April 26, 1971. (Only a few excerpts of this speech were published in the newspapers.)

13. O. Dorticós, "Análisis y perspectivas del desarrollo de la economía cubana," *Economía y Desarrollo*, no. 12 (July-August 1972): 49–53 and "El combustible: factor esencial para el mantenimiento de la actividad económica," ibid., p. 80.

14. F. Castro, "Primera Plenaria Nacional de Producción y Productividad de la Industria de Materiales," transmitted by Radio Havana, December 21, 1971.

15. Orlando Carnota, "El Analista de Sistemas y el Licenciado en Control Económico: profesionales básicos en la informática de gestión," *Economía y Desarrollo*, no. 10 (March-April 1972): 121–34.

16. See interview with Carlos Rafael Rodríguez for the Chilean magazine, *Chile*

Hoy, August 9, 1972, reproduced in *Economía y Desarrollo*, no. 14 (November-December 1972): 154–55.

17. O. Dorticós as quoted by *Latin America* (November 2, 1973): 252.

18. "Proyecto de Resolución acerca de la capacitación cultural y técnica y la formación profesional de los trabajadores," XIII Congreso de la CTC, November 11–15, 1973.

19. "Sistema de Registro Económico," *Cuba Internacional* 5 (February, 1973): p. 8; JUCEPLAN, "Introducción al Sistema de Registro Económico," *Economía y Desarrollo*, no. 15 (January-February, 1973): pp. 7–30; and "El Registro Económico en Minería, Combustible y Metalurgia," *Bohemia* (August 24, 1973): 26–27.

20. Mario Nuti, "Contra la ganancia," answered by Ricardo A. Hernández, "Contra la ganancia: un comentario," *Economía y Desarrollo*, no. 8 (October-December 1971): 3–17.

21. Zoila González Maicas, "Algunas consideraciones acerca de la evaluación de inversiones," *Economía y Desarrollo*, no. 12 (July-August 1972): 150-71. See also Manuel Castro Tato, "Análisis general de las etapas fundamentales de decisión en los proyectos de inversión," ibid., no. 15 (January-February 1973), pp. 30–47.

22. Boris Gorbachov and Olga Darusenkov, "Cuba en la nueva etapa de la construcción socialista," *Ciencias Sociales* (Moscow), No. 3 (1973): 91.

23. "Podemos aumentar la producción," *Bohemia* 62 (May 1970): 32–37.

24. For details see my book, *The Labor Sector and Socialist Distribution in Cuba* (New York: Praeger, 1968).

25. Jorge Risquet, "Comparecencia sobre problemas de fuerza de trabajo y productividad," *Granma*, August 1, 1970, p. 4.

26. O. Dorticós, "Discurso en la inauguración de la Escuela de Cuadros del Ministerio de la Industria Ligera" quoted in "Organización y normación del trabajo en 500 grandes centros industriales," *Granma*, September 16, 1970, p. 5.

27. Information from F. Castro, "Speech at the Closing Session of the National Plenary Meeting of Basic Industry," *Granma Weekly Review*, December 20, 1970, p. 5; "Speech in the Rally to Celebrate May Day," ibid., May 16, 1971, p. 6; and "Speech at the May Day Parade," p. 2; "Primer Encuentro Nacional de Organización y Normación transmitted by Radio Havana, January 24, 1972; and information released in the 13th Congress of the CTC, November 11–15, 1973.

28. Minerva Salado, "El puerto por dentro," *Cuba Internacional* 5 (February 1973): 36–45.

29. See note 27.

30. R. Castro, "Palabras en la clausura del acto de constitución del Sindicato Nacional de Trabajadores Agropecuarios," *Granma*, September 10, 1973, pp. 2–3.

31. See note 27.

32. Dorticós, "Análisis y perspectivas," p. 52.

33. F. Castro, "Discurso en el acto de clausura del XIII Congreso de la CTC," *Juventud Rebelde* (November 16, 1973): 7.

34. "Resolución sobre trabajo de la mujer," XIII Congreso CTC, November 11–15, 1973.

35. Dorticós, "Análisis y perspectivas," p. 38.

36. Recent visitors to Cuba have given contradicting versions on the importance of the black market. In 1969 Gil Green [*Revolution Cuban Style* (New York: International Publishers, 1970), p. 22] could not find evidence of it but René Dumont [*Cuba: est-il socialiste?* (Paris: Seuil, 1970), p. 242] did find it in Havana. In mid-1971 Castro reported that the black market was still operating ["Speech in the Rally to Celebrate May Day," *Granma Weekly Review*, May 16, 1971, p. 6] but a U.S. journalist visiting the island at the time reported that it had virtually disappeared in food but it was still operating in clothing although declining [Joe Nicholson, Jr., "Inside Cuba: A Reporter's Notebook; After Fourteen Years of Revolution," *Harper's* 246 (April 1973): 56].

37. F. Castro, "Speech at the Closing Session," p. 6.

38. Ibid.; "Speech in the Rally," p. 6; and information gathered in Cuba by Lourdes Casal, August, 1973.

39. Nevertheless, families with a per capita income of $25 or less per month were exempted from house rent. *Granma Weekly Review*, January 17, 1971, p. 8.

40. *Latin America* (February 19, 1971): 60; (May 19, 1972): 154–56; and (September 8, 1972): 283; "Incentive Program for Cubans Offers More Goods and Food," *The New York Times*, May 15, 1972, p. 12; and information gathered in Cuba by Lourdes Casal, August, 1973.

41. "Theses of the 13th Congress of the CTC," *Granma Weekly Review*, September 2, 1973, p. 9; and Lázaro Peña, "Main Report to the 13th Congress of Central Organization of Cuban Trade Unions," *Granma Weekly Review*, November 18, 1973, p. 4.

42. Information gathered in Cuba by Lourdes Casal, August, 1973.

43. According to the American journalist, James Higgins, Cuban officials told him in early 1971 that the investment ratio had increased from 31 percent in 1968 to 33 percent in 1970 but declined to 28 percent in 1971. Conversation at Harvard University, May 14, 1971.

44. See note 40; "Cuba: Shadows over Carnival," *Latin America* (July 23, 1971): 239; and *Granma Weekly Review*, December 24, 1972, p. 3.

45. "El cambio de libretas," *Bohemia* 65 (August 31, 1973): 26–31.

46. F. Castro, "Speech at the May Day Parade," p. 3.

47. Castro, "Discurso en el acto de clausura," p. 6.

48. Ibid.

49. Castro, "Speech in the Rally," p. 7.

50. Castro, "Discurso en el acto de clausura," pp. 2, 7, 9.

51. "Theses of the 13th Congress," pp. 8–9. Subsequent references to the Congress proceed from this source unless a specific source is provided.

52. "Proyecto de Resolución sobre Organización del Trabajo y Salarios," XIII Congreso CTC, November 11–15, 1973; and Peña, "Main Report," p. 4.

53. Ibid.

54. "Proyecto de Resolución sobre la Emulación Socialista," XIII Congreso CTC, November 11–15, 1973.

55. See Nicholson, "Inside Cuba," p. 56; and "Proyecto de Resolución sobre la Distribución de Artículos Electro-domésticos," XIII Congreso CTC, November 11–15, 1973.

56. F. Castro, "Speech at the Closing Session," p. 3; "Prime Minister Meets with Representatives from 487 Havana Work Centers," *Granma Weekly Review*, April 25, 1971, pp. 2–3; "Speech at the Rally to Celebrate the 11th Anniversary of the Committees for the Defense of the Revolution," *Granma Weekly Review*, October 10, 1971, p. 3.

57. Ibid.; Radio Havana, several transmissions in late 1971 and early 1972; F. Castro, "Speech in the Rally," p. 4, "Speech at the May Day Parade," p. 2, and "Speech at the International Workers' Day Parade," *Granma Weekly Review*, May 13, 1973, p. 2; *Granma Weekly Review*, August 19, 1973; and "La construcción veinte años despues," *Bohemia* 65 (August 31, 1973): 23.

58. A. MacEwan, "Incentives, Equality and Power in Revolutionary Cuba," paper delivered at Conference of the Union for Radical Political Economics, New York, December 28, 1973, p. 8.

59. Information on sugar in this section comes from *Revolutionary Change in Cuba*, pp. 301–11, several issues of *Granma Weekly Review*, and transmissions from Radio Havana.

60. F. Castro, "Speech in the Graduation of 2,095 Students of the University of Havana," *Granma Weekly Review*, December 17, 1972, p. 9.

61. For a detailed study of voluntary labor in the 1960s see my article, "Economic Significance of Unpaid Labor in Socialist Cuba," *Industrial and Labor Relations Review* 22 (April 1969): 339–54.

62. "Theses of the 13 Congress," pp. 8–9; and "Proyecto de Resolución sobre Trabajo Voluntario," XIII Congreso CTC, November 11–15, 1973.

63. F. Castro, "Speech at the Closing Session," pp. 3–5.

64. *Granma Weekly Review*, December 10, 1972, p. 9 and January 14, 1973, pp. 2–3; José Vásquez, "Cinco preguntas sobre la zafra," *Cuba Internacional* 5 (February, 1973); 16–17; and Marcelo Fernández Font, "The United Nations Conference on Sugar 1973," *Granma Weekly Review*, June 24, 1973, p. 10.

65. Centro de Investigaciones de la Caña, "Efecto de la quema de los campos en la producción de azúcar," *Economía y Desarrollo*, no. 10 (March-April 1972): 92–118.

66. Centro de Investigaciones de la Caña, Centro de Información Científica y Técnica, Universidad de La Habana, *Sistema australiano de corte, zafra 1971* (La Habana: Investigaciones Agrícolas Agroindustriales, Serie 8, no. 8, December 1971) and "Introducción en Cuba del sistema australiano de corte," *Economía y Desarrollo*, no. 15 (January-February 1973): 48–71.

67. F. Castro, "Speech at the Rally to Celebrate the 18th Anniversary of the Attack on Moncada," *Granma Weekly Review*, August 1, 1971, p. 4; "Speech at the May Day Parade," p. 3.

68. O. Dorticós, Radio Havana transmission of July 1, 1972. Two months later the president confirmed his previous statement and said that targets for 1973–1975 had been "more or less quantitatively defined" and that work had begun on the

1976–1980 targets; but he did not release any data on those targets. "Closing Speech at the 40th Conference of Sugarcane Technicians," *Granma Weekly Review,* September 10, 1972, p. 2.

69. *Granma Weekly Review,* May 20, 1973, p. 11.

70. Antonio Núñez Jiménez, "Ceremony Honoring the 10th Anniversary of the Academy of Sciences of Cuba," *Granma Weekly Review,* March 5, 1972, pp. 4–5.

71. The latest statistical yearbook published by Cuba's Central Planning Board, *BE Boletín Estadístico 1970,* includes information only until 1970 and in vital aspects repeats the series of 1962–1966 published in two previous issues. The results of the population census, taken in September, 1970 (the first in 17 years), had not been published by the end of 1973. The Institute for Latin America of the Soviet National Academy of Sciences in a recently published statistical compendium on the nations in the area includes Cuba only in two tables, one on population and another on foreign trade. (Akademii Nauk SSSR, Institut Latinskaia Ameriki, *Latinskaia Amerika i cifras,* Moscow: 1971). For details on Cuban statistical sources and accuracy see my article, "Availability and Reliability of Statistics in Socialist Cuba," *Latin American Research Review* 4 (Spring and Summer 1969): 53–91 and 47–81.

72. Based on JUCEPLAN data and my computations in *Revolutionary Change in Cuba,* pp. 330–31. Cuba's GMP per capita in 1962–1967 declined at an average annual rate of minus 2.6 percent.

73. International Bank for Reconstruction and Development, "World Bank Atlas," *Finance and Development* 9 (March 1972): 58. According to this source, Cuba's GNP per capita in 1960–1969 declined at an average annual rate of minus 3.2 percent.

74. "Cuba," *Barclay's Economic Intelligence Department* (London), December 17, 1971; and "Cuba: From Dogma to Pragmatism?," *Bolsa Review* (London) (April 1972): 197.

75. O. Dorticós, "Control económico y perspectivas del desarrollo de la economía cubana," *Economía y Desarrollo,* no. 11 (May-June 1972), p. 11; and "Desarrollar cultural, científica y técnicamente los cuadros administrativos," ibid., no. 20 (November-December 1973), p. 54; C. R. Rodríguez, "Speech at the 15th Session ECLA in Quito, Ecuador," *Granma Weekly Review,* April 8, 1973, p. 9; and F. Castro, "Discurso en el acto de clausura del XIII Congreso de la CTC," *Juventud Rebelde,* November 16, 1973, p. 6

76. Based on JUCEPLAN data and my computations in "Cuba," *Scholarly Resources Company* to be published in 1974.

77. Nora Frómeta, "Minister of Light Industries Reports on Production for 1971," Joel Domenech, "Basic Industry Production Up in 1971," and "Balance Sheet for 1971: Advances Chalked Up in the Field of Mining, Fuels and Metallurgy," *Granma Weekly Review,* January 30, 1972, pp. 8–10.

78. F. Castro, "Speech at the May Day Parade," p. 2.

79. F. Castro, "Speech at the Ceremony Held to Celebrate the Completion of a Unit of the Electrical Enterprise at Tallapiedra," *Granma Weekly Review,* July 30, 1972, pp. 2–3.

80. *Granma Weekly Review,* January 21, 1973, p. 7; January 28, 1973, p. 5; February 11, 1973, pp. 10–11; February 18, 1973, p. 5; and March 4, 1973, p. 6.

81. Rodríguez, "Speech at the 15th Session of ECLA in Quito, Ecuador," *Granma Weekly Review,* April 8, 1973, p. 9, and "Interview in Hungary," *Granma Weekly Review,* December 16, 1973, p. 10.

83. FAO, *Monthly Bulletin of Agricultural Economics and Statistics* 19 (July-August 1970): 14–17.

84. Informe de la Delegación de Cuba [al] XVI Período de Sesiones de la FAO, *La producción agropecuaria en el II Decenio para el Desarrollo* (Rome: n.p., 1971), pp. 8–9.

85. F. Castro, "Speech at the Closing Session," pp. 3–4; "Speech at the Rally to Celebrate the 18th Anniversary," p. 8.

86. Dorticós, "Análisis y perspectivas," pp. 44–45.

87. *Bolsa Review* (April 1972): 199; *Latin America* (May 19, 1972): 154, and (July 28, 1972): 234–36; and F. O. Licht, July 1972.

88. *Granma Weekly Review,* May 20, 1973, p. 11; and *Latin America* (June 15, 1973): 187.

89. Marcelo Fernández, "Cuba is Interested in Signing an International Sugar Agreement but not Just any Kind of Agreement," *Granma Weekly Review,* December 2, 1973, p. 8. See also "Cuba: Sugar Bonanza," *Latin America* (January 18, 1974): 23.

90. "Cuba: Economic Results in 1972 and Perspectives for 1973," *Comercio Exterior* (Mexico), March 1973.

91. Dorticós, "Análisis y perspectivas," pp. 41–42.

92. "La ponencia de Clark, Willis y Preston sobre los F-1," *Granma Revista Semanal,* May 18, 1969, p. 6; M. B. Willis, "Fertilidad de la vaca de carne," *Revista Popular de Divulgación Agropecuaria* 1 (January-April 1971): 7–22; and various papers published in *Revista Cubana de Ciencia Agrícola.*

93. *Granma,* June 23, 1971, p. 1; F. Castro, "Speech at the Rally to Celebrate the 18th Anniversary," pp. 4–5.

94. Dorticós, "Análisis y perspectivas," p. 42; *Granma Weekly Review,* January 21, 1973, p. 7, and January 28, 1973, p. 5.

95. Ibid.

96. Jorge Risquet, Radio Havana, May 25, 1972. The overall *acopio* rate of increase in 1972 over 1971 was not given, but increases of 108 percent in tubers and 18 percent in fruits and a decline of 17 percent in vegetables were reported. (Nothing was said about tobacco and coffee.) *Acopio* reportedly increased at an overall rate of 10 percent in 1973. "Production by Small Farmers Shows Marked Increase in 1973," *Granma Weekly Review,* March 10, 1974, p. 9.

97. F. Castro, "Speech on the 19th Anniversary of the Attack on the Moncada Garrison," *Granma Weekly Review,* August 6, 1972, p. 7.

98. F. Castro, "Speech at the Closing Session of the 4th Congress of the ANAP," *Granma Weekly Review,* January 19, 1972.

99. F. Castro, "Speech at the Main Ceremony Commemorating the 20th

Anniversary of the Attack on the Moncada Garrison," *Granma Weekly Review,* August 5, 1973, p. 5.

CHAPTER 3

1. For a picture of the Cuban situation in these years, see my essay "Ideological Radicalization and Economic Policy in Cuba," *Cuban Communism,* Irving Louis Horowitz, ed. (New Brunswick, N.J.: Transaction Books, 1972), pp. 93–122.

2. L. Huberman and P. Sweezy, *Socialism in Cuba* (New York: Monthly Review Press, 1969), pp. 201–18.

3. The controversy was published in *Monthly Review* in 1968–1969 and compiled as *On the Transition to Socialism* (New York: Monthly Review Press, 1971).

4. M. Zeitlin, "Inside Cuba: Workers and Revolution," *Ramparts* 8 (March 1970): 20, 70–78.

5. R. Dumont, *Cuba: est-il socialiste?* (Paris: Editions du Seuil, 1970), pp. 134–223.

6. K. S. Karol, *Guerrillas in Power: The Course of the Cuban Revolution* (New York: Hill & Wang, 1970), pp. 329–30, 410, 457–58.

7. F. Castro, "Comparecencia . . . sobre la zafra azucarera de 1970," *Granma Resumen Semanal,* May 31, 1970, p. 12.

8. F. Castro, "Discurso en conmemoración del XVII aniversario del asalto al Cuartel Moncada," *Granma Resumen Semanal,* August 2, 1970, pp. 2–6.

9. J. Risquet, "Comparecencia sobre problemas de fuerza de trabajo y productividad," *Granma,* August 1, 1970, pp. 5–6.

10. F. Castro, "Discurso en el X aniversario de la constitución de la FMC," *Granma Resumen Semanal,* August 30, 1970, pp. 4–5.

11. F. Castro, "Discurso en la plenaria provincial de la CTC," *Granma Resumen Semanal,* September 20, 1970, pp. 4–5.

12. F. Castro, "Discurso en la concentración para celebrar el décimo aniversario de los CDR," *Granma Resumen Semanal,* October 4, 1970, pp. 4–5.

13. F. Castro, "Speech at the Closing Session of the National Plenary Meeting of Basic Industry," *Granma Weekly Review,* December 20, 1970, pp. 2–3.

14. See, for a detailed discussion of this subject, Andrés Suárez, *Cuba: Castroism and Communism, 1959–1966* (Cambridge, Mass.: MIT Press, 1967) and "Leadership, Ideology and Political Party," *Revolutionary Change in Cuba,* Mesa-Lago, ed., pp. 3–21.

15. "Executive Committee of Council of Ministries Established," *Granma Weekly Review,* December 3, 1972, p. 3.

16. B. Roca, "Nuevo sistema judicial," *Cuba Internacional* 3 (November-December, 1971): 72–75.

17. José Gabriel Gumá, "Unification of the Judicial System," *Granma Weekly Review,* September 5, 1971, p. 8. See also Osvaldo Dorticós, "Speech at the

Inauguration of the Council of Government of the People's Supreme Court," *Granma Weekly Review,* July 15, 1973, pp. 4–5.

18. *Prensa Latina* (Havana) July 1, 1971.

19. Gumá, "Unification of the Judicial System," p. 8.

20. Author's estimates based on list published as "Comité Central del Partido," *Verde Olivo* 6 (October 10, 1965).

21. Information released by Raúl Castro, "At the 15th Anniversary of the Triumph of the Revolution," *Granma Weekly Review,* January 13, 1974, p. 3.

22. *Partiynaya Zhizn* (Moscow), April 10, 1973, quoted by George Volsky, "Cuba Fifteen Years Later," *Current History 66* (January, 1974): 11.

23. Ibid.; and O. Dorticós, *Primer Activo Nacional de Educación Interna del Partido* (La Habana: Ediciones COR, No. 16, 1971).

24. Information gathered in Cuba by Lourdes Casal, August 1973.

25. Materials used in these courses were published in numerous issues of *Granma* throughout 1973.

26. Suárez, "Leadership, Ideology and Political Party," pp. 10, 18; F. Castro, "Discurso en el acto de clausura del XIII Congreso de la CTC," *Juventud Rebelde* (November 16, 1973): 10; and R. Castro, "At the 15th Anniversary of the Triumph of the Revolution," *Granma Weekly Review,* January 13, 1974, pp. 2–3.

27. Secundino Guerra Hidalgo, "The Congress: The Party's and the Nation's Most Important and Decisive Meeting" and "The Party Program: Analysis and Objectives for Changing an Objective Reality," *Granma Weekly Review,* December 23, 1973, pp. 8–9.

28. For a detailed study of the role of the armed forces in the 1960s see Jorge I. Domínguez, "The Civil Soldier: The Military as a Governing Institution in Cuba," paper delivered at Inter-University Seminar on Armed Forces and Society, Chicago, October 1973.

29. "Cuba: Discipline and Incentives," *Latin America* (September 21, 1973): 302–303.

30. "Militia Day," *Granma Weekly Review,* April 22, 1973, pp. 1–2, 6–7.

31. Law 1,257, December 1, 1973. See "Law of Council of Ministers on New System of Rank in Revolutionary Armed Forces," *Granma Weekly Review,* December 16, 1973, p. 2.

32. See F. Castro comments on the law, ibid., p. 3.

33. Lionel Martín, "Reestructuración sindical en Cuba," *Cuba Internacional* (April 1971): 28–30.

34. J. Risquet, "Comparencencia sobre problemas de fuerza de trabajo," pp. 5–6.

35. Ibid.

36. F. Castro, "Discurso en la concentración," pp. 4–5.

37. "Acuerdos del Comité Nacional de la CTC" and "Orientaciones para el proceso eleccionario," *Granma,* October 30, 1970, p. 2.

38. Radio Rebelde, transmissions of December 2 and 3, 1970.

39. J. Risquet, "Palabras en la Plenaria Provincial de la CTC," *Granma,* September 9, 1970, pp. 4–5.

40. F. Castro, "Discurso en la concentración," pp. 4–5.

41. *Granma*, October 30, 1972, p. 2.

42. J. Risquet, "Speech at the Closing Session of the 6th National Council of the Central Organization of Trade Unions," *Granma Weekly Review*, October 24, 1971, p. 4.

43. See F. Castro's explanation at the establishment of the National Trade Union of Basic Industry, "Speech at the Closing Session," p. 2.

44. Information from Radio Havana, *Granma* and Castro's speeches especially "Speech at the International Workers' Day Parade," *Granma Weekly Review*, May 13, 1973, p. 5.

45. R. Castro, "Speech at the Closing of the National Conference of Civilian Workers of the FAR," *Granma Weekly Review*, September 26, 1972, p. 5.

46. Martín, "Reestructuración sindical en Cuba," p. 30; and "Cuba: Trade Unions," *Latin America* (July 28, 1972): 234, 236.

47. J. Risquet, "Palabras en la Plenaria," pp. 4–5.

48. J. Risquet, "Speech at the Closing Session of the 6th," p. 4.

49. F. Castro, "Speech in the Rally to Celebrate May Day," *Granma Weekly Review*, May 16, 1971, p. 2; "Speech at the Rally to Celebrate the 18th Anniversary of the Attack on the Moncada," *Granma Weekly Review*, August 1, 1971, p. 1.

50. "Theses of the 13th Congress of the CTC," *Granma Weekly Review*, September 2, 1973, pp. 11–12. Following quotations from and references to the "theses" come from this source.

51. Lázaro Peña, "Main Report to 13th Congress of Central Organization of Cuban Trade Unions," *Granma Weekly Review*, November 18, 1973, p. 4.

52. "Over 1½ Million Workers Participate in Discussion of 9 Theses of 13th Workers' Congress," *Granma Weekly Review*, November 4, 1973, pp. 4–5.

53. "Estatutos de la Central de Trabajadores de Cuba y Declaración de Principios o Fundamentos," XIII Congreso CTC, Havana, November 11–15, 1973, pp. 1–10.

54. Peña, "Main Report to 13th Congress," p. 5.

55. Castro, "Discurso en el acto de clausura del XIII," p. 8.

56. J. Risquet, "Speech at the Closing Session of the 6th," p. 4.

57. "Proyecto de Resolución sobre las Asambleas Regulares de Producción y Servicios," XIII Congreso CTC, Havana, November 11–15, 1973.

58. On the technical advisory councils see Cuban Economic Research Project, *Labor Conditions in Communist Cuba* (Coral Gables: University of Miami Press, 1963), p. 8. On *Poder Local* see González, *Cuba under Castro*.

59. R. Castro, "At the 15th Anniversary," pp. 2–3.

60. Law 1,269 of May 9, 1974. See excerpts in *Granma Weekly Review*, May 19, 1974, p. 1.

61. See N. Kishin, E. Smirnov and A. Bezvenezhnij, "URSS: Los Organos de Poder del Pueblo; estructura y función de los Soviets," *Bohemia* (January 11, 1974), pp. 30–35; and Blas Roca, "Matanzas: Organos del Poder Popular," *Bohemia* (May 3, 1974).

62. J. Risquet, "Palabras en la Plenaria," pp. 4–5 and "En la clausura . . . ," *Granma Revista Semanal*, August 17, 1969, p. 2. See also "Franco debate obrero," *Granma*, September 8, 1970, p. 5.

63. Quotation and information come from J. Risquet, "Speech at the Closing Session of the 6th," p. 4.

64. "A Battle Already under Way," *Granma Weekly Review*, December 5, 1971, p. 1.

65. Law No. 1,225, August 29, 1969; "Proyecto de evaluación laboral," *Granma*, July 8, 1970, p. 1; "Proyecto sobre méritos y deméritos laborales," *Granma*, September 12, 1970, p. 3; and Resolution No. 425, October 15, 1970, *Granma*, October 16, 1970, p. 1.

66. The draft of the law was published in all newspapers in early January, 1971 ("Draft Law against Loafing," *Granma Weekly Review*, January 17, 1971, p. 7.) The draft was to be discussed in meetings by hundreds of thousands of workers, which would "enrich it with numerous, astute observations" ("A Legislative Forum of the Working Class," *Granma Weekly Review*, January 30, 1971, p. 3.). But when the final law was enacted in March there were practically no changes made in the draft (Law No. 1,231, of March 16, 1971, *Granma Weekly Review*, March 28, 1971, p. 2).

67. "Statement by the CTC . . . ," *Granma Weekly Review*, March 28, 1971, p. 2.

68. J. Risquet, "Speech at the Closing Session of the 6th," pp. 4–5.

69. Jesús Montané, "Speech at the National Plenary Meeting of Labor Justice," *Granma Weekly Review*, January 23, 1972, pp. 10–11.

70. "Theses of the 13th Congress," p. 9; and "Proyecto de Resolución sobre la Emulación Socialista," XIII Congreso CTC, Havana, November 11–15, 1973, pp. 3–4.

71. For a detailed discussion of the status of small farmers and rural workers under the Revolution see *Revolutionary Change in Cuba*, chapters 11 and 12.

72. Data on the reduction of the private agricultural sector come from José Acosta, "La revolución agraria en Cuba y el desarrollo económico," *Economía y Desarrollo*, No. 17 (May–June 1973), pp. 155–59.

73. Radio Havana, transmission of March 4, 1971.

74. "Cuba: Trade Unions," pp. 234, 236.

75. F. Castro, "Speech at the Closing Session of the 4th Congress of ANAP," *Granma Weekly Review*, January 9, 1972, pp. 2–4.

76. Radio Havana, transmission of January 13, 1972.

77. Acosta, "La revolución agraria," pp. 158–59.

78. Castro, "Speech at the Closing Session of the 4th," pp. 2–4.

79. Jaime Crombet, "Summary of the Report of the National Committee of the Young Communist League," *Granma Weekly Review*, April 9, 1972, pp. 2–3.

80. Ibid.; and Radio Havana, transmission of March 1, 1972.

81. *Granma Weekly Review*, November 21, 1971, p. 8.

82. F. Castro, "Speech at the Final Session of the 2nd Congress of the Young Communist League," *Granma Weekly Review*, April 16, 1972, pp. 2–4.

83. Ibid.

84. F. Castro, "Speech at the Final Session of the 2nd," pp. 2–4; and Belarmino Castilla, "Speech at the Opening of the National Congress on Education and Culture," *Granma Weekly Review*, May 9, 1971, pp. 4–5.

85. "Declaration by the First National Congress of Education and Culture," *Granma Weekly Review*, May 9, 1971, pp. 4–5.

86. "El Fórum logró acercarnos aún más a nuestro pueblo," *Granma Revista Semanal*, May 11, 1969, pp. 7–10; and F. Castro, "Speech at the Tenth Anniversary of the Creation of the Ministry of Interior," *Granma Weekly Review*, June 13, 1971, pp. 4, 6.

87. Martin Schram, "Cuba Today: Universities 'Open to All,' But . . . ," *Newsday*, September 10, 1971. Mr. Schram visited the university and spoke with students and professors about the incident.

88. "Final Declaration of the 2nd Congress of the Young Communist League," *Granma Weekly Review*, April 23, 1972, pp. 7–8.

89. F. Castro, "Speech at the Final Session of the 2nd," pp. 5–7.

90. Raúl Castro, "Important Battles are Being Waged in the Field of Production," *Granma Weekly Review*, August 12, 1973, pp. 2–3.

91. F. Castro, "Speech at a Ceremony Inaugurating 102 Schools," *Granma Weekly Review*, November 4, 1973, p. 2; and Raúl Castro, "Speech at the Ceremony Marking the Anniversary of the Founding of the UJC," *Granma Weekly Review*, April 14, 1974, pp. 2–3.

92. "Declaration by the First National Congress of Education and Culture," pp. 4–5.

93. Castro, "Speech at the Tenth Anniversary," pp. 4, 6.

94. *Granma*, May 26, 1973.

95. Jesús Montané, "Speech at the Second Party Assembly at the University of Havana," *Granma Weekly Review*, July 11, 1971, p. 4.

96. Joe Nicholson, Jr., "Inside Cuba: A Reporter's Notebook; After Fourteen Years of Revolution," *Harper's* 246 (April 1973): 57.

97. For details on the events of 1959–1970 see the chapters by Lourdes Casal on literature and Julio Matas on cinema and theater in *Revolutionary Change in Cuba*.

98. F. Castro, "Speech at the Closing Session," p. 4.

99. "The Olivé Case," *Granma Weekly Review*, February 21, 1971, p. 7.

100. *Le Monde*, April 9, 1971.

101. F. Castro, "Speech at the Main Event in Commemoration of the Victory of Playa Girón," *Granma Weekly Review*, May 2, 1971, p. 5.

102. F. Castro, "Speech in the Inauguration of a Junior High School in Jagüey," *Granma Weekly Review*, May 2, 1971, p. 9.

103. Padilla's statement of self-criticism was released by the Cuban press agency *Prensa Latina* in Paris. Excerpts were published in *Le Monde*, April 29, 1971, and *The New York Times*, May 26, 1971. The complete text in Spanish was published by *Casa de las Américas* 11 (March-June 1971): 191–203.

104. "Declaration by the First National Congress of Education and Culture," pp. 5–6.

105. F. Castro, "Speech at the Closing of the First National Congress of Education and Culture," *Granma Weekly Review,* May 9, 1971, pp. 7–9.

106. *Le Monde,* May 20, 1971, and *The New York Times,* May 22, 1971. These and other documents are in a compilation by Lourdes Casal, *El caso Padilla: Literatura y Revolución en Cuba* (New York: Ediciones Nueva Atlántida, 1972). For a good analysis see José Yglesias, "A Cuban Poet in Trouble: The Case of Heberto Padilla," *New York Review of Books* (June 3, 1971): 3–8. See also the compilation and debate in *Libre* (Paris), 1 (September-November 1971) and (December 1971-February 1972).

107. F. Castro, "Speech at the Tenth Anniversary," p. 3.

108. Personal information made available to the author in June-December, 1971. Among those rejected were two well-known political scientists and one economist. On the other hand, American experts on education and public health entered Cuba with relative facility.

109. Schram, "Cuba Today: Universities 'Open to All', But . . .".

110. "U.S. Writer Describes Months in Cuban Prison," *Los Angeles Times,* June 13, 1972, p. 4; and Frank McDonald, "Report from a Cuban Prison," Institute of Current World Affairs, several issues from September 1972 to August 1973 (see especially the latter, No. 18, pp. 6–7).

111. Augusto E. Benítez, "Marginality: A Case of Sociological Espionage," *Granma Weekly Review,* March 4, 1973, p. 10.

112. See Virgilio Perera and Leonardo Acosta, "La campaña anti Martí," *El Caimán Barbudo,* No. 65 (February-March 1973): 19–24, and No. 66 (April-March 1973):12–15. In July 1974, however, the Cuban government invited a top Ford official to visit Cuba.

113. "All Cuban Stations Ban U.S. Music," *The New York Times,* April 22, 1973. One year later, however, pop music was back on the Cuban stations.

114. Bettelheim, "La révolution cubaine sur la voie soviétique," *Le Monde,* May 12, 1971.

CHAPTER 4

1. See Ernesto F. Betancourt, "Exporting the Revolution to Latin America," and Irving Louis Horowitz, "The Political Sociology of Cuban Communism," in *Revolutionary Change in Cuba,* pp. 105–41.

2. F. Castro, "Speech in the Ceremony to Commemorate the Centennial of the Birth of V. I. Lenin," *Granma Weekly Review,* May 3, 1970, pp. 2–5.

3. F. Castro, "Speech at the Close of the Main Rally Marking the Beginning of the Ten-million-ton Sugar Harvest," *Granma Weekly Review,* July 20, 1969, p. 5.

4. F. Castro, "Discurso en conmemoración del Centenario del Natalicio de Lenín," *Granma*, April 23, 1970, pp. 2–4.

5. *Granma Weekly Review*, December 26, 1971, and January 2, 1972. In March 1973, Cuba freed one of the two remaining Cuban-born prisoners as a friendly gesture toward Panama.

6. *Granma Weekly Review*, March 25, 1973, pp. 8–11.

7. CORFO, *Chile Economic News* (February 27, 1971): 3.

8. *Granma Weekly Review*, April 1, 1973, p. 8.

9. *Comercio Exterior* (Mexico), March 1972; *Latin America* (March 16, 1973): 83; and *Granma Weekly Review*, June 13, 1973, p. 3.

10. "Caribbean: Cuba Back in the Fold?" *Latin America* (October 20, 1972): 229; *Granma Weekly Review*, December 24, 1972, p. 13, and September 16, 1973, p. 1.

11. *Granma Weekly Review*, May 20 and June 3, 1973, p. 1, and March 10, 1974, p. 2; *Latin America* (August 31, 1973): 280, (December 7, 1973): 387, (March 1, 1974): 66; *Time* (February 11, 1974): 38; and *The New York Times*, April 19, 1974, p. 1.

12. *Granma Weekly Review*, January 7, 1973, p. 8.

13. Cuban exiles reacted negatively to Figueres' suggestions with a few remarkable exceptions, e.g., Castro's former minister of finance, Rufo López Fresquet.

14. *Latin America* (September 7, 1973): 28.

15. Marvine Howe, "Venezuela Opens Cuban Contacts," *The New York Times*, April 22, 1973, p. 17.

16. *Time* (April 16, 1973): 38.

17. F. Castro, "Speech at the International Workers' Day Parade," *Granma Weekly Review*, May 13, 1973, p. 3.

18. *Granma Weekly Review*, July 15, September 16, and October 21, 1973.

19. Cuban relations have not only improved with Latin America but with other non-socialist countries as well. Trade with Japan, France, Italy, Canada, Great Britain, Spain, and Sweden increased notably in 1970–1973, reaching the half-billion peso mark. Cuba imported equipment (for transportation, agriculture, industry, and construction) and received technical assistance and credits from these countries in exchange for sugar, nickel, tobacco, and rum. See *Svea Örnstedt SIDA* (Stockholm), July 15, 1971; "Cuba," *Barclay's Economic Intelligence Department* (London), December 17, 1971; "Cuba: From Dogma to Pragmatism," *Bolsa Review* (London), April 1972; and "Cuba's Links with Nonsocialist World Expanding," *Business Latinamerica*, April 20, 1972. At the end of 1971, Castro stated that Cuba was in the process of overcoming the economic embargo and that the island had a growing foreign market and could sell all that it was capable of producing. *Granma Weekly Review*, November 21, 1971, p. 8, and November 28, 1971, p. 4.

20. "Press Conference with Newsmen from Different Countries," *Granma Weekly Review*, December 19, 1971, pp. 8–9.

21. "Press Conference with Newsmen," ibid., p. 15. Castro also justified (ibid., pp. 13–14) his increasingly good relations with Franco's Spain (with which Cuba signed, at the end of 1971, a new four-year trade and payments' agreement including a most-favored-nation clause) on the basis of Spanish resistance to U.S. pressure to

isolate Cuba in the 1960s. For a detailed account of Castro's 1971 trip to Chile and stops to Lima and Quito, see George W. Grayson, "The Significance of Castro's Trip to South America," *World Affairs* 135 (Winter 1972): 220–39.

22. Hugo Blanco, *Land or Death: The Peasant Struggle in Peru* (New York: Pathfinder Press, 1972), pp. 63, 74. See also "Hugo Blanco Leaves Mexico," *Intercontinental Press*, July 10, 1972.

23. Heinz Rudolf Sonntag, "Discusión con Héctor Béjar," *Libre* 1 (Paris), (March-May 1972): 44–52.

24. *Granma Weekly Review*, November 21, 1971, pp. 9, 12.

25. F. Castro, "Speech at the Farewell Meeting Arranged for him by the People of Chile at the National Stadium," *Granma Weekly Review*, December 19, 1971, pp. 2–4. See also press conference on pp. 9–11.

26. See *Granma Weekly Review*, September 23 and 30, and October 7, 1973. Castro's detailed version of the coup is given in the latter.

27. The only reaction of the Cuban press to some of these problems was "Respuesta a cierta prensa Mexicana," *Granma*, August 18, 1969. See also Patricia Nelson, "Mexican-Cuban Relations," *The Christian Science Monitor*, November 11, 1969, p. 4.

28. *New Nation* (Georgetown), October 14, 1972.

29. *Granma Weekly Review*, September 16, 1973.

30. Cuban reports were published in *Granma Weekly Review*, February 11, 18, and 25; see also *Latin America* (February 23, 1973): 57–58, (June 1, 1973): 176.

31. F. Castro, "Speech at the Close of the Main Rally," p. 5; "Discurso en conmemoración del Centenario," pp. 2–4; and "Speech at the Main Event in Commemoration of the Victory of Playa Girón," *Granma Weekly Review*, May 2, 1971, p. 6.

32. Benjamin Welles, "More Latin Lands Seem Willing to End Ban on Cuba," *The New York Times*, August 14, 1971, p. 3.

33. Ibid.; and "Peru: End of Story," *Latin America* (June 2, 1972): 169–70.

34. "Cuba: From Dogma to Pragmatism"; and "Cuba and the Recent Vote in the OAS," *Granma Weekly Review*, June 18, 1972, p. 12.

35. Galo Plaza's statement was made on April 26, 1973 at the Conference "The OAS Today and Tomorrow" at the University of Pennsylvania, Philadelphia.

36. F. Castro, "Speech at the International Workers' Day Parade," pp. 2–3.

37. See *The New York Times*, April 19, 1974, pp. 1, 12 and May 6, 1974, p. 8. *Granma* reported the event in a responsive manner. See *Granma Weekly Review*, April 28, 1974, p. 12.

38. For example, the 1968 conversations between Antonio Núñez Jiménez, President of the Cuban Academy of Sciences, and American intellectuals who tried to facilitate the interchange of scholars and publications; the 1968–1969 agreements of the Hispanic Foundation, Library of Congress, and of the Latin American Studies Association in order to promote intellectual interchange; the seminars held in 1968–1969 by the Center for Inter-American Relations (CIAR) of New York with the purpose of recommending to the U.S. government a new policy with respect to Cuba;

and the 1969 Ford Foundation grants made available for field research in Cuba. See also the articles by John N. Plank, "We Should Start Talking with Castro," *The New York Times Magazine,* March 30, 1969, p. 29; Irving Louis Horowitz, "United States-Cuba Relations: Beyond the Quarantine," *Trans-action* (April 1969): 43–47; Richard Fagen, "United States-Cuban Relations," *Contemporary Inter-American Relations: A Reader in Theory and Issues,* Yale H. Ferguson, ed. (New York: Prentice Hall, 1972), pp. 192–203 (this is Fagen's report to the CIAR meetings of 1968–1969); and Jorge I. Domínguez, "Taming the Cuban Shrew," *Foreign Policy,* no. 10 (Spring 1973): 94–116.

39. For background on U.S.-Cuban relations see Cole Blasier, "The Elimination of U.S. Influence," *Revolutionary Change in Cuba,* pp. 43–80; and Edward González, "The United States and Castro: Breaking the Deadlock," *Foreign Affairs* 50 (July 1972): 722–37.

40. For instance Robert A. Hurtwitch in February, 1970 in the television program "The Advocates," in July, 1970 before the House Foreign Affairs Committee, in September, 1971 before the Senate Foreign Relations Committee, and in February, 1973 before the Congress; a State Department report to the OAS in March, 1970; Secretary Rogers to the Congress in March, 1971; Charles Appleton Meyer to the press in July, 1971; and President Nixon to the press in April, 1971 and January, 1972.

41. *Granma Weekly Review,* December 26, 1971, and January 2, 1972.

42. Tad Szulc, "U.S. Government Scientists Attended Parley in Cuba," *The New York Times,* July 11, 1972.

43. *Granma Weekly Review,* February 25, 1973, p. 3.

44. Castro, "Speech in the Main Event," p. 6.

45. *Granma Weekly Review,* December 19, 1971, pp. 10–13; and George Natanson, "Nixon Doesn't Represent World Realities—Castro," *The Times of the Americas,* May 13, 1972, p. 2.

46. *Granma Weekly Review,* June 4, 1972, p. 6. Two weeks later the Cuban press mentioned conditions 3 and 4 ignoring the first two. In October, Castro mentioned conditions 1 and 2 ignoring the last two. In December he ignored condition 1 (the end of the war in Vietnam was in sight) and seemed willing to yield on condition 4. In May, 1973 he definitely dropped condition 1, reiterated 2 and 3 (although changing their order, therefore giving priority to a domestic matter over an inter-American issue) and said that condition 4 was still on but had a lower priority.

47. F. Castro, "Speech on the 19th Anniversary of the Attack on the Moncada Garrison," *Granma Weekly Review,* August 6, 1972, p. 6.

48. In late 1973 the Soviet press clearly indicated that a Cuban rapprochement with the United States would be welcome: "Even in the United States, sober voices of politicians and public figures are raised increasingly about the need to reexamine U.S. relations with Cuba. . . . Cuba's peace-loving foreign policy is convincing proof of its desire to live in peace and friendship with all peoples, above all with the peoples of Latin America." *Izvestia,* September 8, 1973, as quoted by George Volsky, "Cuba Fifteen Years Later," *Current History* 66 (January 1974): 14, 35. Reviewing Brezhnev's visit to Cuba in 1974, TASS stated: "Many observers hold the view that

the visit will bring about a thaw in the political climate of the Western Hemisphere." Quoted by *Latin America* (February 8, 1974): 47.

49. Some of these problems were briefly explained by Castro, "Speech at the Main Event," p. 6.

50. *Latin America* (October 20, 1972): 229; and (January 25, 1974): 26.

51. "Memorandum of Conversation [of Bill Post] with Zenen Buergo Concepción at Cuban Mission to the U.N.," January 11, 1974.

52. "Cuba: Brezhnev's Visit," *Latin America* (February 1, 1974): 36; and *The New York Times*, February 5, 1974, p. C-3.

53. "Bienvenido Brezhnev," *Time* (February 11, 1974): 37–38. The possibility of a U.S.-Cuban rapprochement generated a curious movement in U.S. financial circles: old Cuban railroad bonds went up as much as 400 percent and some Cuban government bonds that were recently selling at about 10 percent of their face value went up as much as 50 percent. *The Times of the Americas*, February 6, 1974, p. 12. The Cubans also showed interest: an official at the UN Mission asked whether any U.S. banks or other corporations desired détente with the island, and if so, why and which corporations these might be. "Memorandum of Conversation," p. 2.

54. *The New York Times*, February 21 and 25, 1974, pp. C–14 and C–3.

55. See *The New York Times*, January 9 and 11, 1974 and the second week of January issues of *The Miami News* and *The Miami Herald*. Surprisingly, Ambassador López retracted his statement in an interview with Miami Spanish-language radio station WFAB which is partly owned by Cuban exiles.

56. "Congressional Conference on U.S.-Cuban Relations," Washington, D.C., New Senate Office Building, April 19–20, 1972.

57. *Latin America* (February 13, 1973): 64.

CHAPTER 5

1. I used a primitive version of such a model, for the first time, in the final chapter of the book I edited, *Revolutionary Change in Cuba*, pp. 510–24, to describe and analyze the feasibility of alternative paths that were open to Cuba in 1970. My prediction that Cuba would probably follow the Economic-Reform Soviet system has been confirmed by recent history and documented in this book. An improved version of my model was published as "A Continuum Model to Compare Socialist Systems Globally," *Economic Development and Cultural Change* 21 (July 1973): 573–90. This work stimulated me to organize in Pittsburgh in 1972–1973 an international seminar on the "Methodology to Compare Socialist Systems." Papers presented in that seminar, including a substantially enlarged version of my own model will be published in 1975 as *Comparative Socialist Systems: Essays on Politics and Economics*, Carl Beck and Carmelo Mesa-Lago editors.

2. For a full discussion of this hypothesis see my article "A Continuum Model to Compare Socialist Systems Globally," pp. 586–87.

3. In the remainder of this section the causes of the 1970-on Cuban movement

toward the center and pole Y are analyzed. For an abstract discussion of the causes of gravitation of socialist systems toward one pole or its opposite in the continuum see my contribution to *Comparative Socialist Systems: Essays on Politics and Economics* forthcoming.

4. The study was conducted by Luigi R. Einaudi (now Kissinger's advisor on Latin American affairs), Edward González, and David F. Rondfeldt. See González, *Cuba Under Castro*, p. 226.

5. The continuation of Cuban dependency regardless of the change in ideology and association presents a challenge to the theory of *dependencia* developed by Latin American and North American social scientists. Helio Jaguaribe has articulated this point: "The transition of Cuba to socialism resulted in this country's independence vis-a-vis the United States but undoubtedly created a broad and noticeable dependency upon the USSR. . . . A country cannot break away from dependency through a mere change in its system [or ideology] but a feasible transformation of its structure is required ["national viability"]. Cuba lacked the conditions to undertake the latter due to the island's isolation and insufficient natural and human resources, therefore, its dependent status has persisted." See "La América Latina ante el siglo XXI," *El Trimestre Económico* 41 (April-June 1974): 425. For more details see Helio Jaguaribe, *Political Development: A General Theory and a Latin American Case Study* (New York: Harper & Row, 1973).

Index